ALBERT FREY

ALBERT FREY

inventive modernist

EDITED BY BRAD DUNNING

RADIUS BOOKS

PALM SPRINGS ART MUSEUM

This publication was made possible with the support of its title sponsors, Roland Lewis and Michael Noll.

previous page:

Frey at the drafting/dinner table,
Frey House II (1963)

photographer unknown
ARCHITECT: Albert Frey
Palm Springs Art Museum
Albert Frey Collection, 55-1999.2, VIIC59

opposite:

LANCE GERBER

Frey House II (1963)

photographed 2023
ARCHITECT: Albert Frey
Courtesy of Palm Springs Life

following spread left:

MODEL

Aluminaire House (1930)

made by Albert Frey
photographer unknown
ARCHITECTS: A. Lawrence Kocher with Albert Frey
Palm Springs Art Museum
Albert Frey Collection, 55-1999.2, VIIA7-29

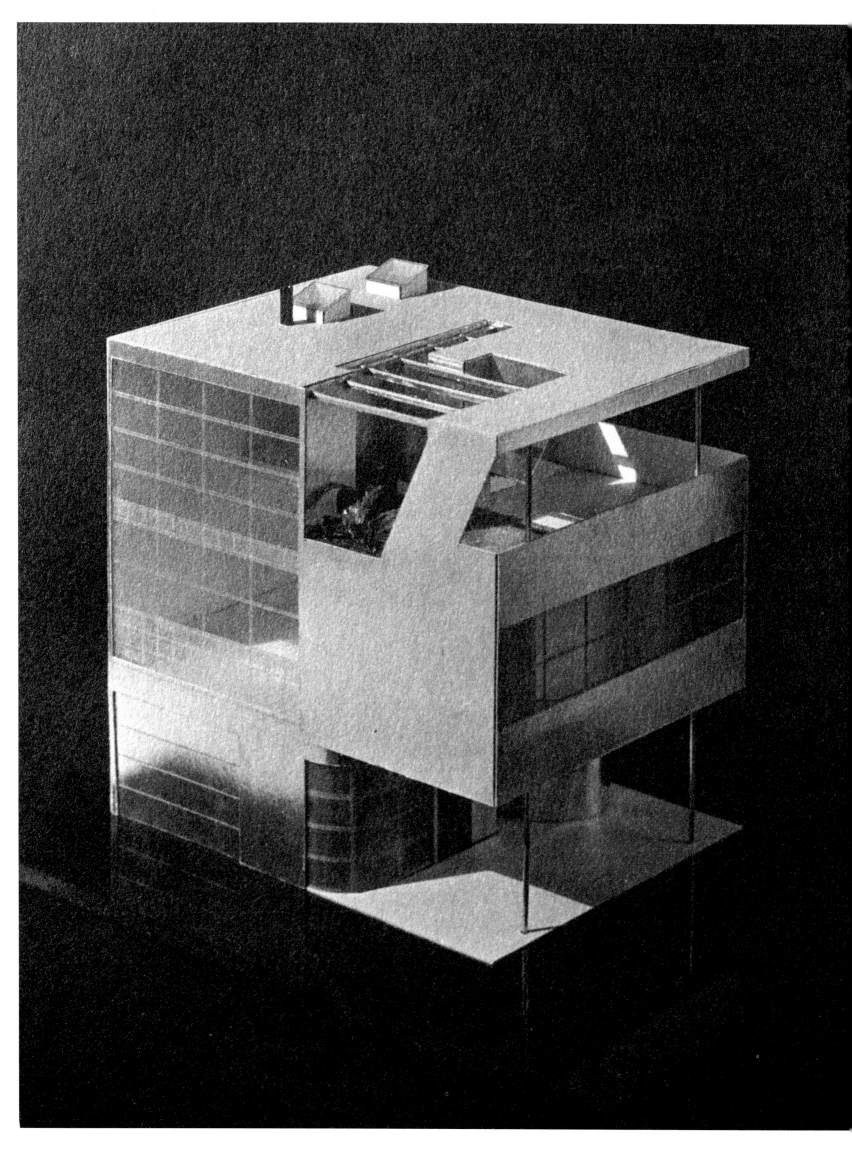

CONTENTS

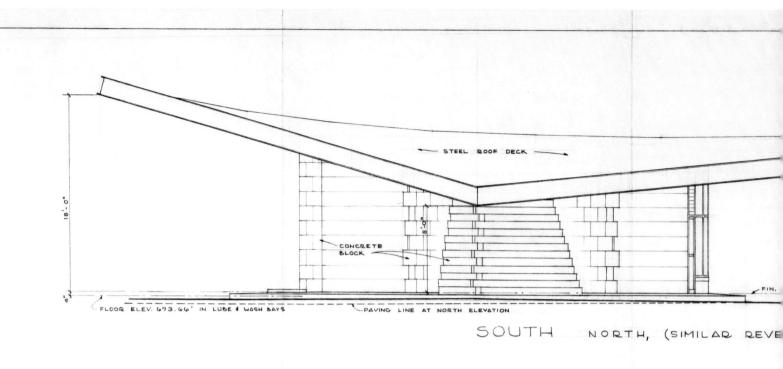

STEEL ROOF DECK

18'-0"

8'-0"

CONCRETE
BLOCK

4"

FIN.

FLOOR ELEV. 673.66' IN LUBE & WASH BAYS

PAVING LINE AT NORTH ELEVATION

SOUTH   NORTH, (SIMILAR REVE

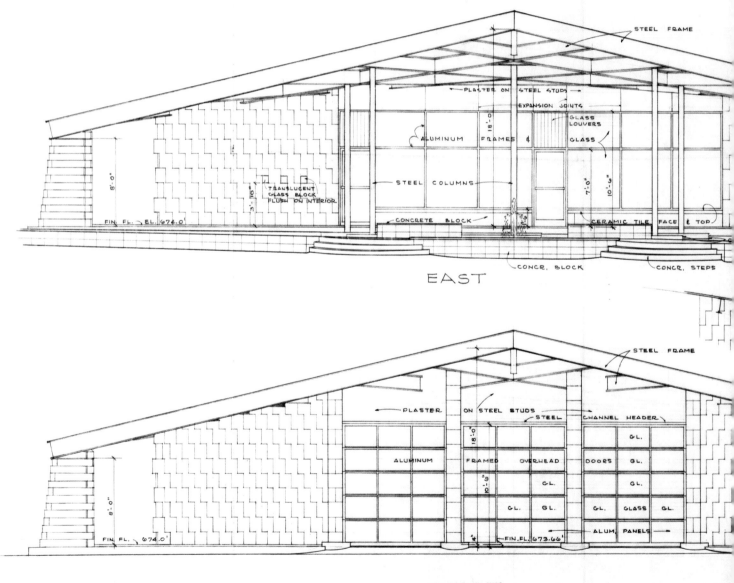

STEEL FRAME

PLASTER ON STEEL STUDS

EXPANSION JOINTS

GLASS
LOUVERS

ALUMINUM   FRAMES &

GLASS

18'-0"

STEEL   COLUMNS

TRANSLUCENT
GLASS BLOCK
FLUSH ON INTERIOR

3'-10"

8'-0"

FIN. FL. EL. 674.0'

7'-0"

3'-10"

CONCRETE   BLOCK

CERAMIC TILE FACE & TOP.

CONCR. BLOCK

CONCR. STEPS

EAST

STEEL FRAME

PLASTER   ON STEEL STUDS

STEEL   CHANNEL HEADER

18'-0"

GL.

ALUMINUM   FRAMED   OVERHEAD   DOORS   GL.

3'-10"

GL.

8'-0"

GL.   GL.   GL.   GLASS   GL.

FIN. FL.   674.0'

FIN. FL. 673.66'

ALUM. PANELS

WEST

EXTERIOR ELEVATIONS SCALE 1/4" = 1'-0"

The ocean liner *SS Bremen* was the fastest, most technologically advanced transatlantic carrier of its time. Its sleek design featured a streamlined, aerodynamic profile. And it was fast—this "greyhound" of the sea, able to cross the Atlantic in just five days, the most modern ocean liner of its time—speed being that great signifier of the twentieth century. Hence, it is more than appropriate that architect Albert Frey chose this mode of transportation when he immigrated to the United States in 1930.

Frey was an ambassador, a disciple, and an emissary, bringing with him on that fateful voyage the teachings and philosophies of his mentor, Le Corbusier, in whose office he had worked, absorbing and learning from the master that creative force of purism, brutalism, and sculptural genius. When Frey stepped off that ship in New York, he was the first employee and student of Le Corbusier to physically and intellectually piggyback Corbusien architectural modernity to the United States.

All the architectural cognoscenti in Manhattan and the world paid close attention to Le Corbusier's architectural innovations and every move. With his association, Frey quickly found employment on the East Coast, soon partnering with architect and editor A. Lawrence Kocher on the design for the famous Aluminaire House (1930) (PP. 42–51) and other noteworthy projects, four of which were built, others not. In Frey's early American period, the Corb influence was strong and inescapable; the young Frey was still firmly under the transatlantic spell of his master's voice. For instance, the Aluminaire House bears an uncanny resemblance to Le Corbusier's Maison Citrohan (1922). In other early projects, such as the Kocher Canvas Weekend House (1934), one can see Frey channeling his bespectacled guru as well.

In an uncanny twist of cosmic synchronization and fate, Frey found his way to the far-flung desert hinterland of Palm Springs (population 1,433 at the time) to monitor a beautiful—and still very Corbusien—building for Kocher's brother, the first resident doctor in Palm Springs. With the Kocher-Samson building of 1934, Frey was the first strict modernist to build in Palm Springs. He survived the locals' shock of the new at this usual modern style and paved the way for the many modernist architects and designers in the area who came after.

Frey eventually decided to stay in the Palm Springs for the rest of his life; he had fallen in love with the desert, turning down offers in New York that would have given him greater income and his work much wider exposure. I love him for that.

Eventually, with time's passing and more understanding of his new geographical location, Frey moved out of the shadow of Le Corbusier and into the harsh sunshine of the desert and his own style, but he never forgot the philosophy and artistry, absorbed into his DNA, espoused by Corb. Palm Springs became Frey's scintillant, his magnificent desolation, his sandy blank canvas.

Frey interpreted International Style modernism into his own unique brand, a combination of the pragmatic and artistic. He defied taxonomy—his best work is seemingly uncategorizable. At different times, he could be described as a minimalist, a constructivist, an expressionist—yet he was always modern, embracing new materials at every turn. He had an unquestionable belief in the future and in beauty and utility.

His final home, known internationally as Frey House II (1963) (PP. 144–161), was the culmination of his career. There, it all came together—design, site, materials, colors—a nearly sacred consecration to architecture and nature, his two great loves.

As an architect, Frey was both part of and separate from Palm Springs. He literally rose above it with Frey House II, high on the hill, where he lived out his remaining days receiving visitors, feeding his animal friends, overlooking his canvas, and watching the town below grow. He had a quiet, mannerly magnetism that drew people to him, and he was hardly a hermit, as is often thought. Instead, he took great delight and joy from the students, fans, and visitors who made their way up the hill to see him. He seldom strayed from his hilltop aerie, his own private terrestrial paradise of heroic purity where he pursued the exquisite beauties of nature and architecture until his death.

It is difficult to convincingly group Frey with the other esteemed architects who make up what is now known as the "Palm Springs School." Frey might have been playful in his constructions and materials, but he was never martini-ed or kitschy in any way. He was also, by far, the most democratic of all the Palm Springs architects, always concerned with low-cost housing and how to enhance a simple home with good ideas and materials. Throughout his career, he would devote as much time and attention to large commercial and civic projects as he would to just about anyone who wanted him to remodel their bathroom, closet, kitchen, or outdoor BBQ area. He wanted to work, and he wanted to show that good design could be achieved on any budget for any person.

He left behind a lot that matters. One building by Frey in some other town would be cause for celebration. Palm Springs is so full of them, it may not completely appreciate the bounty. With *Albert Frey: Inventive Modernist*, I strive to show not only the justifiably well-known projects but countless other works that Frey was able to inject with his unique design aesthetic, clever and artful compositions, and experimentation with new materials. Albert Frey pursued a lifelong quest for the regality of order and for the harmony of the manmade with the natural.

— BRAD DUNNING

PARADOX
OF INFLUENCES

Paul Goldberger

Any discussion of Albert Frey needs to begin with a paradox: he is the architect who, more than any other, is the symbol of Palm Springs, whose buildings have played a critical role in giving the city its design identity, and yet, at the same time, his architectural roots could not be farther from the desert. Frey was born and educated in Switzerland; he did not see the United States until he immigrated to New York in 1930, and it was 1934 before he first arrived in Palm Springs. After an early interlude in Brussels, his architectural career began in earnest with a stint in the atelier of Le Corbusier in Paris. After he came to the United States, he remained devoted to Le Corbusier, who he considered his mentor, and became, for all intents and purposes, Corbusier's first American acolyte.

Frey's career in many ways would be an attempt to resolve the conflict between his Corbusian roots and his American surroundings. He would remain loyal to both, and if the setting for almost all his notable work would be the un-Corbusian environment of the California desert and mountains, he would adapt his sensibility to the easy, more indulgent nature of Palm Springs without ever abandoning the rigor and the directness of his master. His work would never flirt with frivolity, like much of the mid-century architecture that is identified with Palm Springs, yet compared to the architecture of Le Corbusier, Frey's buildings are relaxed, even loose, and seem to revel in hints of exuberance. For Frey, the notion of an understated exuberance was not an oxymoron; it was a governing precept.

Frey's most important early work in the United States, the Aluminaire House (PP. 42–51), is clearly Corbusian, at least in appearance: crisp and modern, taut and light, a house built to assure its occupants a continuous sense of connection to the sun and fresh air (Frey would say that he coined the name to make clear the connection of the design to both its metal cladding and to the open air). It was, in a sense, more Corbusian than Corbusier, since it was designed to be prefabricated out of aluminum panels, a material that was not central to Corbusier's vocabulary, and its blunt, matter-of-fact façade—more boxy than elegant—was even more austere than the exteriors of Le Corbusier's houses of the same period, such as the Villa Savoie and the Maison LaRoche. The Aluminaire's real debt is to Corbusier's Maison Citrohan, his prototype for a modest, easily reproducible modern house that was first developed in 1920, refined over the years, and built in a fully realized version in Stuttgart, Germany, in 1927.

The building in Germany was conceived as part of an international exhibition of modern architecture orchestrated by Mies van der Rohe, and it had a parallel in the circumstances for which the Aluminaire was designed: a public exhibit produced jointly by the Architectural League of New York and the Allied Arts and Building Products Exhibition, for which A. Lawrence Kocher, with whom Frey had been working since his arrival in New York, had been asked to come up with a design that would attract the attention of the general public. Kocher and Frey, perhaps mindful of the full-scale buildings that had been constructed for the German exhibition, suggested constructing an entire house for the week-long exhibition and convinced the Aluminum Company of America and other manufacturers to donate materials.

The Aluminaire, Frey's first building in the United States, would have an extraordinary history. It fulfilled its purpose and became the object of significant press attention, both positive and negative (it was called the "the canned house" by the *New York Sun*), and it was one of only two American houses included in Henry-Russell Hitchcock and Philip Johnson's landmark exhibition of 1932 at the Museum of Modern Art that introduced the International Style to the United States. Hitchcock and Johnson heightened the innovative credentials of the house by describing it as "an experimental house with a skeleton of aluminum and with walls thinner than are permitted by urban building laws." At the conclusion of the exhibition, the house was purchased by the architect Wallace K. Harrison, who used it as a guest house on his weekend estate on Long Island, but by the 1980s, it had fallen into disrepair and was almost demolished by a subsequent owner of Harrison's property. After an outcry from historic preservationists who were only beginning to come to terms with the notion that there was modern architecture old enough to qualify as historic and good enough to be worth preserving, it was moved to the campus of the New York Institute of Technology, where it remained for several years. In 2017, the original pieces of the house were shipped across the country to the Palm Springs Art Museum, which, in a gesture that unites the East and West Coast portions of Frey's career, plans to re-erect Aluminaire on its campus adjacent to the museum's main building.

The Aluminaire House was a spectacular debut for a young architect—Frey was twenty-seven when it was designed—but it did not portend a long partnership with Kocher, a committed modernist who was more successful at writing and editing (he was the managing editor of *Architectural Record*) than he was at getting clients. Frey moved in and out of Kocher's office in response to the sketchy flow of work and, at one point in early 1934, went to Washington, DC, on a three-month assignment from the United States Department of Agriculture to work on its Farm Housing Project, which created prototypes for small houses that farmers could erect at a low cost. Frey, characteristically, produced a scheme for a flat-roofed structure of corrugated metal that was altogether different from any of the other prototypes, which were traditional cottages.

Frey's design underscored his determination at that point in his career to be experimental, to bring many of Le Corbusier's ideas about industrial materials to the United States, and to seek ways in which architectural innovation might serve people at every economic level. He followed the Department of Agriculture project with a project of his own he called the "Subsistence Farmhouse," and conceived numerous other experimental houses, most of which were unbuilt. He later worked with Kocher on Kocher's own weekend house on Long Island that would be sheathed in canvas, blurring the distinction between formal and casual, between indoor and outdoor, and between public and private space. It was effectively a summer pavilion on Corbusian pilotis. One of the few actual paying commissions Kocher received was the call to design a small office building for his brother, a doctor in Southern California who had decided to relocate to Palm Springs, and late in 1934, Frey went to the desert to supervise construction. It would turn out to be a monumental turning point in Frey's career. Although he would return both to Europe and New York for brief periods, including a stint in 1938 to work with Philip L. Goodwin on the original building of the Museum of Modern Art, Frey took so quickly to the desert that Palm Springs became his home for the rest of his life.

In 1935, Frey wrote to Le Corbusier, who was visiting New York, in the hope of enticing him to California. "The east coast of the U.S. is still quite European, enlarged to grotesque proportions," Frey wrote. "It is in the new towns Out West, established during the evolution of the automobile, where modern American life is found. In Los Angeles. . .the town is spread out, not concentrated, it's true, but one travels at 40 km and traffic keeps moving." He described Palm Springs as "a winter resort for the elite in business, industry, and the intellect, it provides the rare pleasure of combining a magnificent natural environment with being a center for interesting and varied activities. Moreover, the sun, the pure air and the simple forms of the desert create perfect conditions for architecture."

Frey was clearly smitten. The mountains reminded him of Switzerland, and the culture of the West seemed much more open to new ideas than that of the East. Still, much of the resort architecture of Palm Springs at that point was traditional, and it is not impossible that the small desert city could have developed into another Santa Barbara or Palm Beach, places in which the taste preferences of the rich for some variation of Spanish Mediterranean or Spanish Colonial architecture became all but mandated as a local style. Frey would have none of that, obviously, and his arrival in Palm Springs was more than a piece of good fortune for himself; it was also a fortuitous event in the city's architectural history, since Frey arrived during the Depression, when building was slow, and in the mid-1930s, traditional architecture, however common, had not yet become as firmly established in Palm Springs as it was in Santa Barbara. There was room, in other words, for something else.

That something else—the modernism of Palm Springs—would be created by many architects over the three decades that followed Frey's arrival, but Albert Frey was arguably its primary catalyst, the architect who would jump-start the movement with his initial project, the Kocher-Samson building, a rigorous, sharp-edged, white building of the International Style on North Palm Drive in the city's modest business district. It was a stake, a modernist marker thrown down in the center of town. Frey was not the first to design modern buildings in Palm Springs, but he was the first modernist architect to come from elsewhere and decide to settle in Palm Springs to see what he could make of it, and what it could make of him. He quickly formed a partnership with John Porter Clark, a local architect who was open to modern design; the two became friends and built houses next to each other, and Frey's residence became an essential calling card for their practice.

Before he arrived in Palm Springs, Frey's work was largely disconnected from place. The Aluminaire House was quite literally unrelated to any site; it was designed to be assembled anywhere, and it had no relationship to context, climate, landscape, or street. Frey's early interest in prefabrication and industrial form seemed to transcend the notion that architecture can be the expression of a particular place, if not even to contradict it. And Frey's other early projects were generally modernist objects more than they were responses to the conditions of specific communities: the tightness and austerity of the Kocher-Samson Building, for example, has more in common with the white International Style buildings in Holland and Germany that filled Hitchcock and Johnson's book than it does with other buildings in Palm Springs. It was not hard to see that it had been designed in New York by an architect who had received his training in Europe from a celebrated International Style master.

That would change quickly as Frey, enamored of the desert as he had been of no other place, at least in the United States, began to think about his architecture in terms of where it was as much as in terms of what it was. He did not give up his commitment to industrial form, to crisp modern lines, and to most of the other elements that had characterized his work. But his modernism began, slowly, to loosen, to be a bit more indulgent and less stern. Frey would never be an architect of hedonism, or even one who designed with any great degree of wit, but his work became more picturesque, more flowing, more accepting of pleasure. It was a transformation that was subtle but powerful. He held on to those aspects of the International Style that worked in the desert environment, like the clean lines and flat roofs and the easy communication between inside and outside, but Frey added to these a degree of emotion that had not been visible before. His work began to relax, and he moved away from thinking of his designs as prototypes that would demonstrate a vision for fixing the world and toward seeing them as buildings that would fulfill simpler programs and enrich the nature of the town to which he had staked his future.

We can see the evolution beginning in that first house Frey designed for himself in 1940 (Frey House I [PP. 88–105]). A composition of sliding planes, with lots of glass, it seems more Miesian than Corbusian, even lighter than his earlier work, almost a simple version of the Barcelona Pavilion turned into a desert pavilion. Openness to landscape and light is all. In a 1945 house and guest house for the actor Raymond Hatton, Frey explored the Barcelona Pavilion again; wing walls extend the wall planes of the structures into the landscape, and the two houses—the guest house a slightly smaller version of the main house—play off and against each other in the desert landscape. The following year, Frey's house for one of his most famous clients, the industrial designer Raymond Loewy, was more expansive and even a bit playful with elements like a pool that crossed the boundary between inside and outside. Here, the pavilion grew more substantial at no loss to its lightness and connection to the desert landscape. In another house, which calls to mind the second Herbert Jacobs House by Frank Lloyd Wright, Frey experimented with a curving floor plan.

By the time Frey expanded his own house for the second time in the early 1950s (he had first added to it in 1948), he had moved far enough away from Corbusian rigor to design the second floor in the form of a cylindrical bedroom with enormous round window openings, an element that looks like an exaggerated industrial object, though Frey reportedly claimed that he was inspired both by the bedroom within the dome of Thomas Jefferson's Monticello and by the observatory tower at the Mayan ruin of Chichen Itza.

The architectural historian David Gebhard, not convinced, referred to the new version of the house as "Frey's Flash Gordon house," and the critic Alan Hess called it "a science-fiction tank. . .a declaration of a new world," and wondered whether Frey had been influenced by the nearby presence of the Edwards Air Force base, where the sound barrier had been broken just a few years before. Whatever his influences, he was clearly no longer constrained by Le Corbusier: Palm Springs and the desert had liberated him.

But to become what? Frey lined the walls of the new tower bedroom with yellow tufted vinyl fabric and designed drapes of electric blue vinyl; elsewhere in the house, he suspended a round dining table from the ceiling with aluminum rods.

If nothing else, Frey, like so many architects both before and after him, was using his own house as a laboratory with which to experiment with design ideas that might be too extreme for clients. But if he was no longer fully in thrall to Le Corbusier, neither did he ever rebel fully against his mentor. For the most part, Frey's work remained spare and carefully composed; its new looseness never seemed superficially decorative, and little in his architecture overtly compromised Le Corbusier's principles. His work was becoming the architectural expression of a community built for leisure and of his own increasing emotional connection to a powerful landscape of desert and mountains, which took it somewhat away from its Corbusian beginnings, but Frey's inherent restraint and his disinclination to excess assured that it would not drift too far from its aesthetic origins.

It is tempting to say that Frey's goal of maintaining his commitment to modernist idealism while at the same time expressing the pleasures, not to say the flamboyance, of Palm Springs was inherently contradictory: there was, after all, a notable puritanical streak to the utopian ambitions of European modernism, and it was surely at odds with the relaxed and indulgent atmosphere of Palm Springs. Frey resolved the contradiction, I think, by turning to the desert itself. As a landscape, the Coachella Valley within which Palm Springs sits is strong, beautiful, and unyielding; its power resists trivia, and its majesty makes the superficially decorative seem trite. Not every architect designing modern buildings in postwar Palm Springs saw this, and many preferred to play to the jauntiness that Palm Springs was coming to acquire in the middle of the twentieth century. But Frey's inclination was to be more serious and to aspire to something noble. In Europe, and in his early American years on the East Coast, he did it by trying to carry forward the potent, if stern, architecture of Le Corbusier. In Southern California, it would not be the force of Corbusier's ideas that energized him but the mountains and the desert spread beneath them. At no point in his career could Frey bear to make architecture that might be considered superficial: it had to be worthy of Le Corbusier, or of the mountains, or both.

It was in restraint, we might say, that the power of his architecture lay, even though in Palm Springs he would be bold in a way that he had not been before. But if his forms were more striking, not to say more expressionist, they never became fussy. His architecture became more inventive as time went on, and surely more distinctly his own, but it always remained clear and direct in a way that separated him from most of his architectural colleagues in modern Palm Springs. The second house Frey designed for himself, finished in 1964 and perched on the mountain above downtown Palm Springs, makes the point. It is a glass pavilion built around an enormous boulder, which defines much of the interior space, a presence on both sides of a glass wall in the same way that the swimming pool in Frey's house for Raymond Loewy was on both sides of an exterior wall.

Frey House II (PP. 144–161), as the house is known, is a tiny masterpiece, a house in the form of an extended balcony over the city. It is at once spare and explosive, and it tries, more literally than anything else Frey designed, to make the desert landscape not merely something to be viewed from the house but a part of the architecture itself, forcing the occupant to engage with it. The house is a kind of skybox, small and tight, looking out across the playing field of Palm Springs; it protects, but even more, it reveals. It is, to offer up another oxymoron, a transparent cave.

Beginning in the 1940s, Frey was commissioned to design several schools in Palm Springs and the surrounding region, and they are all remarkable exercises in desert modernism: spare, tensile, serene, yet full of energy, Barcelona pavilions rendered in inexpensive materials and stretched horizontally to achieve civic scale. It was a time when Le Corbusier was moving toward the heavy, poetic masonry of works like the Maisons Jaouol outside of Paris; Frey went in the opposite direction toward a clean, simple lightness, more Miesian than Corbusian but more Californian than anything else.

There were more civic buildings, including the Palm Springs City Hall, built in stages in 1952 and 1957, where Frey found himself a way to be more expressive than in the schools, if just as conscious of a tight budget. The building is made largely of concrete block in the color of the desert, set with unusual projecting corner details that give it a strong texture, and with two major entrances set off by complementary porticos: a main entrance with a circle cut out of its roof through which three palm trees grow and a freestanding round portico leading to the city council chamber, the diameter of which is identical to the circle cut out of the main portico. Frey extended the circular motif with a series of steel cylinders assembled in rows along a breezeway in front of the building, providing both sun protection and an added rhythm to the façade. It is a building both casual and dignified, a combination that is more notable because its dignity connects so naturally with its informality. The City Hall possesses the easy and informal air of much of the city's mid-century architecture, elevated to civic, if hardly monumental, scale.

Frey may well have come the closest to achieving monumentality in Palm Springs in his only work in a building type that rarely aspires to architectural distinction, let alone achieves it: the gasoline station he designed in 1963 for Enco on Highway 111 at the entrance to Palm Springs, with its soaring, cantilevered roof of galvanized metal that appears almost to be taking off from the base of its concrete block structure and rising to become an exclamation point in the sky. It is Frey's most structurally daring work, not to mention his most high-spirited, and at the same time, it is one of his sparest and most disciplined, its exhilarating form perfectly balancing emotion and intellect and thus, in a sense, bringing the two aspects of Frey's career together. Bought by the City of Palm Springs in 2002 and now serving as a visitors' center, it is the city's true architectural gateway, an architectural shooting star that sums up Frey's career with a burst of optimism. It has rightly become a symbol of the city, a signpost to the world that the desert has brought forth a modernism that builds on what has come before and makes it Palm Springs's own.

FOREWORD

Excerpted from *Architecture and the Decorative Arts* (1988) by Cynthia Zignego Stiverson

Albert Frey

In early September 1930, I arrived in York City via Ellis Island from Zurich, Switzerland, the place of my birth. As a young architect, my hope was to find employment with a firm involved in the new modern style of design. During my first week in New York, I visited serval architects whose work, as described in magazines I had seen, showed a modern trend. This search led me to A. Lawrence Kocher at the offices of *Architectural Record*.

Mr. Kocher proposed that I move in with him and his wife, Amy, at their house on Park End Place in Forest Hills Gardens on Long Island. A bedroom and a bath was available for me as well as an adjacent workroom. In addition to these accommodations and most of my meals, Mr. Kocher offered me a generous $25 per week. He told me that his parents were also of Swiss origin.

During discussions on modern architectural design, Lawrence told me that his extensive research on important traditional buildings, particularly vernacular American structures, convinced him that in each period technical proficiency and modes of living were fundamental in determining the design of buildings.

Gerhard Ziegler, who had collaborated with Kocher on several projects, had left New York before I arrived. Ziegler and Kocher had designed a modern architect's office for the Architectural Arts Exposition at Grand Central Palace in New York City in the spring of 1930. The exhibit had attracted crowds of visitors during the week-long event. I admired the practicality and novel design of a desk made of a chromium plated steel frame with black "Bakelite" top and shelves, which now graced Lawrence's *Architectural Record* office.

As managing editor of the *Architectural Record*, Lawrence Kocher assembled a progress-oriented research and writing staff. They were up-and-coming young men, such as Knud Lonberg Holm, Theodore Larson, and Robert L. Davison. Ernest Born contributed graphic layout and covers. The office was visited by many noted architects and photographers. I recall meeting Luis Barragan, the architect from Mexico City who was beginning to build outstanding houses and developments.

Kocher's sponsorship of modern architecture through the pages of the *Architectural Record* was fraught with many obstacles. The circulation department received letters of disapproval of Kocher's policy from reactionary practitioners in the architectural profession. Editor Michael Mikkelsen was, however, most supportive of Kocher's management.

Mr. Sweat, manager of the Grand Central Palace Exposition, proposed that Mr. Kocher design and build another attention-getting exhibit for the Architectural League Show in the spring of 1931. Lawrence and I had been discussing the need for low-cost housing in those Depression years. We thought that a small, single-family house, using the new methods of prefabrication and maintenance-free materials, would be both popular with visitors to the Exposition and offer a solution for the housing shortage of the times.

Lawrence and I collaborated on articles for the *Architectural Record* concerning low-cost housing. Lawrence's office was part of the F. W. Dodge Corporation, which also produced Sweet's Catalogs, and therefore, he was informed of the latest developments in construction materials and techniques.

We called the house we designed for the League Exposition "Aluminaire," expressing our design concept of light and air. The house would feature large windows and open-air living, and be a durable structure with siding of aluminum. We incorporated many new features and conveniences into the design, such as tubular lighting, compact wardrobes, washable wall surfaces, a stainless steel sink, built-in radio, overhead garage doors, and many more. I made a ¼"scale model of "Aluminaire," and we presented it to the Exposition authorities and to suppliers and manufacturers of materials and products that would be incorporated into the house. Since times were slow, these firms were most cooperative and supportive in donating their services and products. Since there was only ten days between exhibitions at Grande Central Palace, all parts of the three-story "Aluminaire House" had to be pre-fabricated for quick erection. It was very exciting to be on the job and help direct the assembling of the various components. The large attendance at the Exposition and the interest shown by the public and the press was most gratifying and very pleasing to the Exposition management.

After the Exposition, Lawrence and I followed the re-erection of the "Aluminaire" at the estate of Wallace Harrison on Long Island. We took construction snapshots, and had F. S. Lincoln take exterior photographs of the again completed house. Now, fifty-seven years later, it is wonderful that the "Aluminaire" is being reconditioned and re-erected again, this time for good, on the Long Island campus of the New York Institute of Technology.

Lawrence Kocher was a great teacher, and the articles we wrote together for the *Architectural Record* helped me tremendously with learning to express myself in English. He also taught me to drive his air-cooled Franklin convertible. We enjoyed outings, some with his wife who was unfortunately ailing. One memorable trip was visiting Rex Stout in his new house. Another was a trip to Washington, DC, to install an exhibition on contemporary architectural features and to attend President Hoover's Conference on Housing. Yet another was a trip to the site of the future Ralph-Barbarin House in Stamford, Connecticut. Special treats were duck farms or shore restaurants. For recreation and exercise, Lawrence played some golf and tennis, and we would take walks along the beaches and the woods of the island, where he found the site for the future canvas-covered weekend house he would build near Northport, Long Island. In a portion of the basement of his house, he made a game room large enough to play ping-pong. Lawrence was also a member of the Salmagundi Club in New York City. Once he participated in a sailing regatta from New York to Bermuda.

In 1932, while continuing to live and collaborate with Lawrence Kocher, I started to work afternoons with the architect William Lescaze, and I was able to buy a Model A Ford convertible. Driving into New York from Forest Hills, I could park near Lescaze's office at the east end of 42nd Street near the river where the United Nations buildings are now located.

Wanting to discover more about America, I took a camping and photographic trip during July and August of 1932 with a companion Lawrence found for me at the F. W. Dodge Corporation. We drove to Chicago and Wisconsin, where I visited Frank Lloyd Wright at Taliesen. Then on to the wonders of Yellowstone Park, Yosemite, and San Francisco. Driving south, I visited the Kocher house in San Jose, and was greatly pleased to meet Lawrence's mother and other members of the family. In the Los Angeles and San Diego areas, I met the modern architects whose work was being published in the *Architectural Record*, including Schindler and Neutra. On the return trip, I marveled at the Grand Canyon of Arizona, the Mesa Verde Cliff Dwellings in Colorado, and the Indian Pueblos of New Mexico. Then we proceeded south to New Orleans and along the charming Gulf Coast to historical St. Augustine. Driving north, we passed through storied Savannah and Charleston, the tobacco auction towns and Richmond, and finally back to New York and the Kocher home in Forest Hills. Lawrence and I continued to collaborate on articles, furniture designs, and building projects, and I was able to be with Lawrence for the private funeral services after the death of his wife, Amy.

Early in 1933, my oldest sister and her husband asked me to design a modern house for them near Zurich. Since Kocher and I had no immediate or pressing projects, I accepted the challenging invitation and spent nine months in Switzerland. During that time, I wrote two articles for the Swiss architectural magazine *Werk*, illustrating them with photographs of the Kocher and Frey buildings and from my 1932 American trip. During this period, Lawrence married Margaret Taylor, and I was happy to be invited to join them in Forest Hills on my return in October 1933.

The research and projects Lawrence and I had done on farm houses led to a stint at the US Department of Agriculture in Washington, DC, from January through March 1934. There, I designed minimal houses for farmers that they could build with the help of a carpenter—wood-frame buildings with flat roofs and corrugated metal siding.

Returning to Forest Hills, Lawrence and I started on the design and construction of his vacation house. We spent many enjoyable weekends instructing and helping the workers. There were also the happy events of the birth in 1934 of the Kocher's daughter, Sandra, and in 1936, of their son, Lawrence.

Lawrence and I had found that, while metal construction was accepted and competitive in industrial buildings, in houses, particularly in the country where contractors and carpenters were accustomed to wood framing and siding, the new methods were resisted, and costs were increased. Since the Ralph-Barbarian House had to be built within a set budget, we decided to adhere to the building methods of the locality. In designing the house, we provided the ladies with the desired comforts of space and convenience—first-floor garage, storage and entry, second-floor living room, dining room, and kitchen, and third-floor bedrooms and baths with balconies. The house was concrete block at ground level, with shingle siding above and canvas covered decks.

Lawrence Kocher had a brother in Palm Springs, California, named John Jacob Kocher, M.D. He was the first and only physician practicing in the early years of the little desert village situated below the 10,000-foot San Jacinto mountains. Dr. Kocher visited Lawrence during the summers, and he asked him to design a modern office and apartment building for Palm Springs. We started the sketches, and I left for California with the preliminary drawings in late October, 1934. I drove first to Pittsburgh, where I stopped by the H. H. Robertson Company to finalize the layout of their structural steel decking material that we were proposing for the second floor and roof of the building.

In Palm Springs, I found Dr. Kocher most understanding and supportive of our innovative design, and it was a great pleasure to follow through with the detailing, contracting, and supervising the construction. A nephew of the

Kochers was an engineer with the Truscon Steel Company, which furnished the spiral stair, steel studs, and windows. I kept Lawrence informed of the progress with snapshots as the building grew and with professional photographs upon its successful completion. My stay and architectural practice in Palm Springs continued with local architect John Porter Clark. I kept in touch with Lawrence Kocher, sending him documents on projects and finished buildings which he published in the *Architectural Record*.

In 1937, I accepted the invitation of Philip Goodwin to join his firm, which, with Edward D. Stone, had been selected as architects for the new Museum of Modern Art building in New York City. Having enjoyed my years of living in Forest Hills with Lawrence Kocher, who still resided there with his wife, Marge, and daughter, Sandra, I rented a nearby apartment. We continued our friendship and discussions on architecture and many other subjects, and we collaborated on some projects, including a design proposal for the Swiss Pavilion for the 1939 New York World's Fair. Willliam Lescaze, originally from Geneva, was the successful competitor.

Having experienced the natural beauty and healthy life in California, and with Lawrence Kocher planning to leave the *Architectural Record* and New York, I returned to Palm Springs in the fall of 1939 after completion of the Museum of Modern Art and my engagement with Philip Goodwin.

A. Lawrence Kocher went on to Charlottesville, Virginia, then to Black Mountain College in North Carolina, and finally to Williamsburg, Virginia, where he died in 1969. I established an architectural practice in Palm Springs. While our careers diverged after 1939, we always kept in touch. From my first arrival in America in September 1930, I enjoyed and benefited from my wonderful friendship with Lawrence Kocher. His kindness and guidance helped me find my way from then on.

page 8 and opposite:

DRAWING

Service Station for Culver Nichols (1965)

ARCHITECTS: Frey & Chambers
Palm Springs Art Museum
Albert Frey Collection, 55-1999.2, VIIIG1

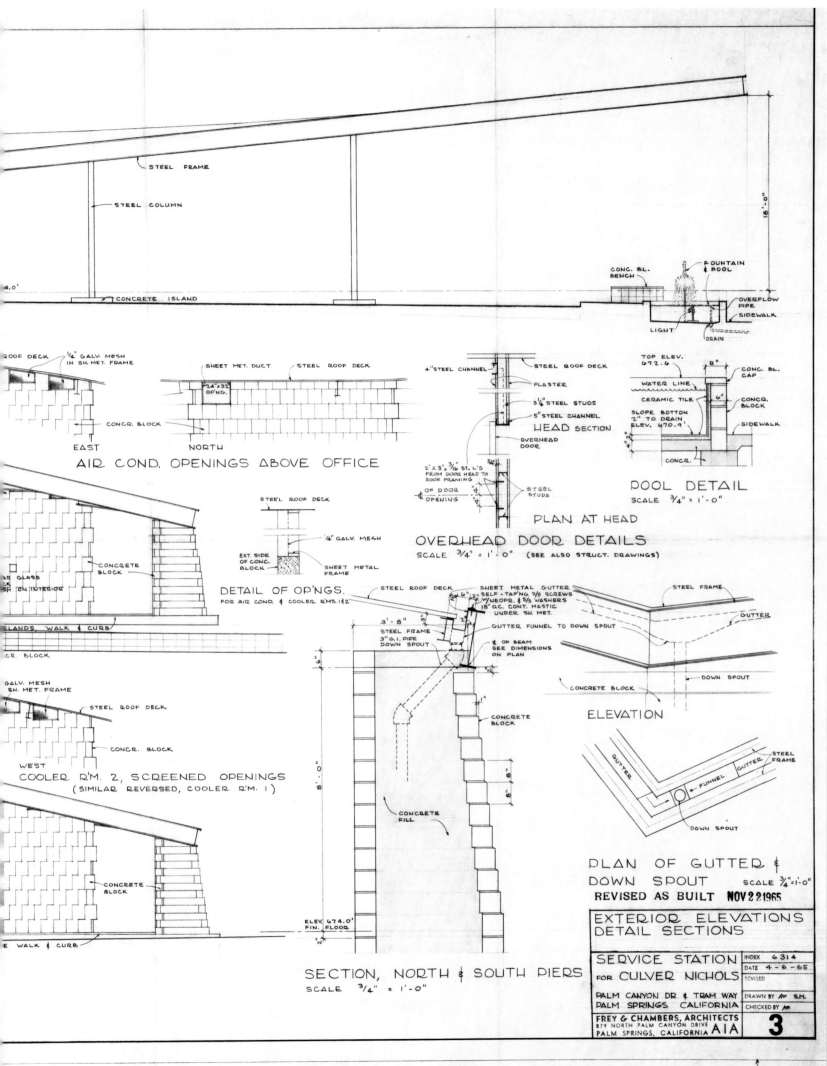

STEEL FRAME

STEEL COLUMN

CONCRETE ISLAND

4.0'

18'-0"

CONC. BL. BENCH

FOUNTAIN & POOL

OVERFLOW PIPE

SIDEWALK

LIGHT

DRAIN

ROOF DECK

¼" GALV. MESH IN SH. MET. FRAME

SHEET MET. DUCT

STEEL ROOF DECK

24"×32" OP'NG.

CONCR. BLOCK

EAST

NORTH

AIR COND. OPENINGS ABOVE OFFICE

4" STEEL CHANNEL

STEEL ROOF DECK

PLASTER

3¼" STEEL STUDS

5" STEEL CHANNEL

HEAD SECTION

OVERHEAD DOOR

2'×3"×³⁄₁₆ ST. L'S FROM DOOR HEAD TO ROOF FRAMING

¢ OF DOOR OPENING

STEEL STUDS

PLAN AT HEAD

OVERHEAD DOOR DETAILS
SCALE ¾" = 1'-0" (SEE ALSO STRUCT. DRAWINGS)

TOP ELEV. 672.6

8"

CONC. BL. CAP

WATER LINE

CERAMIC TILE

6"

CONCR. BLOCK

SLOPE BOTTOM 2" TO DRAIN ELEV. 670.9

SIDEWALK

4'-2"

CONCR.

POOL DETAIL
SCALE ¾" = 1'-0"

STEEL ROOF DECK

CONCRETE BLOCK

AIR GLASS ON INTERIOR

¼" GALV. MESH

EXT. SIDE OF CONC. BLOCK

SHEET METAL FRAME

DETAIL OF OP'NGS.
FOR AIR COND. & COOLER R'MS. 1 & 2

ISLANDS, WALK & CURB

CR. BLOCK

STEEL ROOF DECK

SHEET METAL GUTTER

¼" 6" SELF-TAP'NG. ⅝ SCREWS W/NEOPR. & ⅝ WASHERS 18" O.C. CONT. MASTIC UNDER SH. MET.

STEEL FRAME

GUTTER

3'-8"

STEEL FRAME 3" G.I. PIPE DOWN SPOUT

GUTTER FUNNEL TO DOWN SPOUT

¢ OF BEAM SEE DIMENSIONS ON PLAN

DOWN SPOUT

GALV. MESH SH. MET. FRAME

STEEL ROOF DECK

CONCR. BLOCK

WEST

COOLER R'M. 2, SCREENED OPENINGS
(SIMILAR REVERSED, COOLER R'M. 1)

CONCRETE BLOCK

CONCRETE BLOCK

ELEVATION

GUTTER

FUNNEL

GUTTER

STEEL FRAME

DOWN SPOUT

PLAN OF GUTTER & DOWN SPOUT   SCALE ¾"=1'-0"
REVISED AS BUILT NOV 22 1965

6"

8'-0"

CONCRETE BLOCK

CONCRETE FILL

1"

ELEV. 674.0' FIN. FLOOR

CONCRETE BLOCK

SECTION, NORTH & SOUTH PIERS
SCALE ¾" = 1'-0"

EXTERIOR ELEVATIONS DETAIL SECTIONS

SERVICE STATION FOR CULVER NICHOLS

PALM CANYON DR & TRAM WAY PALM SPRINGS CALIFORNIA

FREY & CHAMBERS, ARCHITECTS 879 NORTH PALM CANYON DRIVE PALM SPRINGS, CALIFORNIA AIA

INDEX 6314
DATE 4-6-65
REVISED
DRAWN BY AF S.M.
CHECKED BY AF

3

PRINT SIZE 24×42 TRIM LINE

PROJECTS | 1925-1997

WITH EXTENDED CAPTIONS BY BRAD DUNNING

According to the architecture magazines that Albert Frey saw as a young man, architects in Belgium were embracing new modern philosophies, and so that is where he decided he should be. Through the architect Victor Bourgeois, Frey was directed to the Brussels firm of Eggericx and Verwhilgen, where he was employed at two different times. This photograph was taken in 1930, shortly before he immigrated to the United States. At Eggericx and Verwhilgen, Frey worked on innovative housing projects in Europe and the Belgian Congo.

When Frey was in university, he discovered the work of the great Swiss architect Le Corbusier, who became his hero. Le Corbusier was doing very interesting, internationally important, and new modern work at the time. Frey discovered his work through the influential book *Towards A New Architecture*, which was so important to him that he kept a copy in his personal library for the rest of his life.

Frey was determined to meet the famous architect. In 1928, he traveled to Paris, and on his very first morning there, he knocked on the door of his hero's studio and was greeted by Pierre Jeanneret, Le Corbusier's cousin, who ran the office. When Frey asked for a job, they told him they did not have any money and could not hire him. Frey said it didn't matter. He wanted to learn from Le Corbusier, and he would work for free if he had to. They told him to come back and to start the next day. Instantly, he was at ground zero for the modern architectural movement, and he proved himself so talented and worthwhile that they eventually paid him a small salary; in fact, he would be one of only two paid employees for almost a year.

Frey working at the office of
Eggericx and Verwilghen, Brussels, 1930

Although his tenure at the famed Le Corbusier atelier was short (1928-1929),
Frey was greatly influenced by his idol and teacher. While at the studio,
Frey would also work alongside such modern pioneers as Charlotte Perriand,
José Luis Sert, and Kunio Maekawa, who would be a lifelong friend.

Frey at Le Corbusier's office, New Year's Eve, 1928

from left to right: Ernest Weissman, Le Corbusier, Nikolai Kolli,
Albert Frey, P. Nahman, Charlotte Perriand, Pierre Jenneret
photographer unknown
Palm Springs Art Museum
Albert Frey Collection, 55-1999.2, VIIC77-3

While at the Le Corbusier atelier, Frey would work on various details of the famed Villa Savoye. Frey's contributions to one of the world's most important modern houses included engineering on the large and heavy sliding glass doors at the rooftop terrace and the rigid tiled chaise lounge in the bathroom, similar ergonomically to the fixed poolside versions he would include in both of his Palm Springs homes.

Soon after his 1930 arrival in New York, Frey was hired by the influential architect and *Architectural Record* magazine editor, A. Lawrence Kocher, an apostle of modernism who was impressed with Frey's talent and tenure with Le Corbusier.

Prefabricated housing greatly interested both Kocher and Frey. When Kocher was invited to present a project for the Architecture and Allied Arts Exposition of 1931, Frey became the lead designer. Kocher was well connected and contacted advertisers and building materials manufacturers, convincing them to donate the materials needed for the "Aluminaire House," the first modern, all-metal house in the United States designed to show the possibilities of affordable, mass-produced, factory-made housing with modern materials.

The 1,200-square-foot, three-story house was a sensation—over 100,000 people toured it in the one week it was on display, and the house was one of the few American projects to be featured in Philip Johnson and Henry-Russell Hitchcock's groundbreaking and influential exhibition *International Style Since 1922* at the Museum of Modern Art in New York City.

Moved, disassembled, and reassembled multiple times over the decades, the "Aluminaire House" is now on display and part of the permanent collection of Palm Springs Art Museum.

Aluminaire House (1930)

photographer unknown
ARCHITECTS: A. Lawrence Kocher with Albert Frey
Palm Springs Art Museum
Albert Frey Collection, 55-1999.2, VIIA7-24

MODEL

Aluminaire House (1930)

made by Albert Frey
photographer unknown
ARCHITECTS: A. Lawrence Kocher with Albert Frey
Palm Springs Art Museum
Albert Frey Collection, 55-1999.2, XVB31

42

4/10/30

PRELIMINARY SKETCH

Aluminaire House (1930)

pencil on paper
ARCHITECTS: A. Lawrence Kocher with Albert Frey
Special Collections, John D. Rockefeller Jr. Library
The Colonial Williamsburg Foundation
A. Lawrence Kocher Collection, MS1986.12

Aluminaire House (1930)

on the campus of the New York Institute
of Technology, Islip, NY, c. 2006

ARCHITECTS:
A. Lawrence Kocher with Albert Frey
Courtesy of Jon Michael Schwarting

Section
IV

INI
AV
AUTC

EIGHT PAGES

Aluminu
Model Str

**Metal and Glass Dwelli
of Ultra-Modern Conce
tionBuilt for League Sh**

Home Built in Full S

**Equipped With New Id
for Contemporary Livi**

By Lloyd Jacquet

Man must have sensed a keen enj
ment when he contemplated his
crudely built house fashioned of sti
hides and grass. It was his creat
erected in record time as construc
work goes nowadays, even in the s
plest cases.

Today man stands before a mode
ized version of this early shelter.
stead of saplings, aluminum bea
animal skins replaced by metal sh
ing; glass supplanting grass; these
the things out of which the cont
porary house—built in one of the m
exhibits of the Architectural Lea
show in Grand Central Palace last w
—is made of.

No mere model, this. Instead, a f
size, three-story building, erected co
plete from plans in a little more th
a week; equipped with a practical
rage, an interesting living room, a
ferent kitchen, and an unusual b
room, besides a sun-terrace and a sn
library that can be turned into ano
room. Practical in the extreme,
not freakish—merely convenient
common sense.

Metallic Framework

As one sees the framework with
sturdy aluminum beams interconne
with the shining columns that sup
the entire structre, the ensemble
angle-irons, steel floors, metal st
cases, window casements, and per
ated uprights give the impression
the interior of a dirigible in const
tion. As the men at work asser
the various numbered units as
workers on skyscrapers do, one gat
the impression that they are enjo
this quite as much as they did put
together the structural toy of
boyhood days.

Visitors will see the effect of
rapidly executed conception of a
temporary home. From the out
though there will not be much op
tunity to get the full effect withln
exhibit hall, the impression is stri
Aluminum metal facing, slightly ri
to break the glare and to accommo
contraction and expansion in va
temperatures, gives it a certain
siveness free from heaviness. A
insulation backs this aluminum sk
ing, and the whole is hung from
framework. This aluminum, and
glass of the windows that are pier
in all but one facade, provide the
exterior surfaces.

No Basement Provided

Though there was no possibilit
a cellar on the exhibition floor in
case, this presented no problem
the house itself when finally er
at some point on Long Island af
has been dismantled following its
play here, will also be built wi

NEW YORK
Herald Tribune
SCIENCE
FEATURE ARTICLES
RADIO NEWS—PROGRAMS
Section
IV

SUNDAY, APRIL 19, 1931   *   EIGHT PAGES

House at Architects' Show Marks New Building Era
...re Designed to Harmonize With Modern Mechanical Progress

Conceived for present-day living requirements, this house, designed and erected under the supervision of A. Lawrence Kocher, architect, disregards all orthodox methods of construction. It is one of the features of the Architectural League Show, which opened in New York yesterday.

Walls and Floors Hung From Metallic Framework, Like Skyscraper Construction

No Basement Is Provided

Multiple-Purpose Rooms Increase Layout Facilities

to the sky. Here one can enjoy sun or shadow, take a sunbath in complete privacy and sleep under the stars on warm summer nights. Under the covered part is placed a dining table adjacent to the dumb-waiter, which brings the food direct from the kitchen below. This table may be folded up and put out of the way when the entire terrace space is required for dancing, games or as a play space for children. A radio connection supplies music. The terrace floor is covered with resilient asphalt tiles—an ideal paving for playing children. Under the part open to the sky is a sunny patch of green grass, unframed by spacious flower boxes, which, with their colorful combinations, contribute to the making of the terrace, one of the most livable places of the house. The architects have not hesitated to expose the roof framing above the roof garden. The structural channels necessary for the construction are exposed in a truthful manner in contrast with the usual pergola beams of wood used on many picturesque old-home imitations. The supports for the terrace roof frame the view in three directions.

First All-Metal House

The house is built with exterior walls of aluminum (the first all-metal house attempted in America) and has insulation that makes the three-inch thick exterior more effective than the usual 13-inch wall of masonry. The house is constructed of materials readily available as standard and in a manner that is a complete departure from tradition. It neglects all of the styles of the past in the attempt to attain convenience ease of living, attractiveness of outlook and a logic of quiet and pleasant existence. It is as if architects had entirely forgotten the manner of building of the past centuries and were interested in creating a needed American house that would be most efficient and with most appropriate materials.

There are no supporting outside walls, as is the case with the usual brick-dwelling. The supports are six slender columns of aluminum that are within the area of the house. These columns uphold cantilever beams from which the outside walls are suspended. It is a new construction that has many advantages. The windows may come where they are needed for daylighting the interior. Inside walls may be placed where wanted.

The structure of the house is largely of aluminum beams or girders that in turn support the deck floor, insulated and surfaced with the rubber and linoleum flooring. To be sure, the house is fireproof and of extreme lightness. Even though the entire construction members were of steel, the total weight would be one-twelfth the weight of the usual house built with concrete and steel.

...sement. The heating system and garage are placed on the ground ... and the cost of excavating is thus ...

...is places the main living rooms ...e the ground level. This part of ... house is reached by means of a ...t flight of stairs, and, because of ...osition, receives all the light and ...that is needed. Extending across ... width of the house and with one ... glazed from floor to a ceiling ...ht of seventeen feet, a clever du-...effect is achieved which increases ...practicability.

...t the other end is a dining-area ...ch can, if desired, be converted into ...tional living-space. The dining-...e when not in use may be con-...ted to the dimensions of a side ...e. This is done by means of an ...enious construction: the table-top, ...ch is rubber-surfaced, is made to ... on a cylinder in the manner of a ...dow-shade. This large room is ...minated by neon lighting, with tubes ...t parallel the head of the window so ...t with reflectors the night-lighting ...s source corresponds to daylighting.

By the turn of a dial one can obtain a clear white light that suggests the quality of daylight or an ultra-violet light or a selection of color.

Located to the right of this living-room combination, and separated by a folding partition are the bedroom, exercise room and bathroom. With the partition swung back, one has the effect of a window running the entire length of the side—22 feet long.

This layout permits of an intensely individualistic arrangement of units. For example, the two beds suggested are placed at right angles to each other; the closets are small, but distinctly masculine or feminine, as the case may be. Although there are actually three rooms here, one room may be made out of this multiple-room suite, with the attendant advantages of ample space for circulation and enjoyment.

There is a door access to the dumb-waiter for sending the laundry bag to the lower floor. The dressing-table is built against the wall and is supported by brackets. It has its justified place under the window where there is a most advantageous light. The mirror placed in front of the window reflects a shadowless face. The moving partition between bed and exercise-room follows a curved line, in order to make the exercise-room more spacious.

The man sitting all day in his office finds in this exercise room the necessary apparatus for gymnastic compensation. A cabinet of aluminum-framing with translucent panels incloses the closet. It is ventilated directly to the exterior with forced draft by a vent pipe with electric fan. The bath tub is partly hidden beyond this toilet cabinet. The wash basin is placed under the window with the mirror in front of it, to again attain a shadowless lighting.

Above the dining space is the library. It occupies about half the area of the living room and is lighted by skylight, which was chosen as most desirable and restful for reading. The room is furnished with a couch, a built-in bookcase, a wall case, also for books, constructed entirely of glass. The library leads on to the roof terrace.

More than half of the ground area covered by the house is regained by means of a flat roof which serves as a luxurious garden terrace. This roof garden is partly covered and partly open

ALUMINAIRE

A House for Contemporary Life

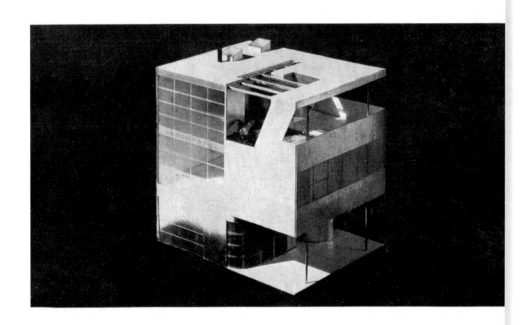

THE ARCHITECTURAL AND ALLIED ARTS EXPOSITION

•

Grand Central Palace, New York City

•

April 18th to 25th, 1931

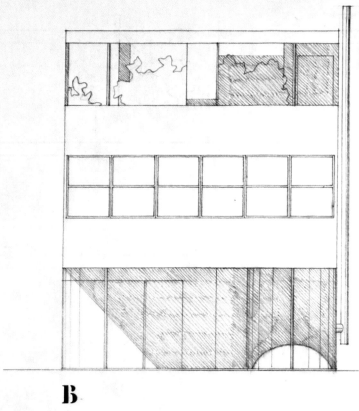

B

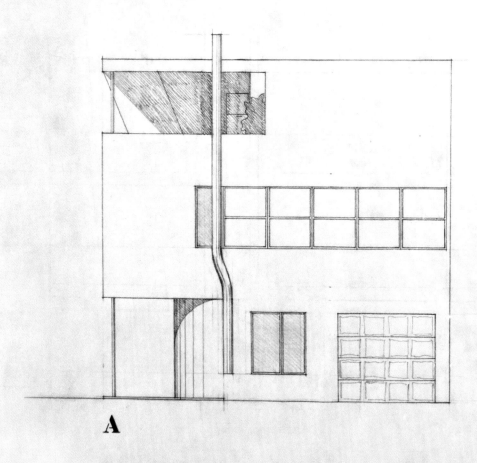

A

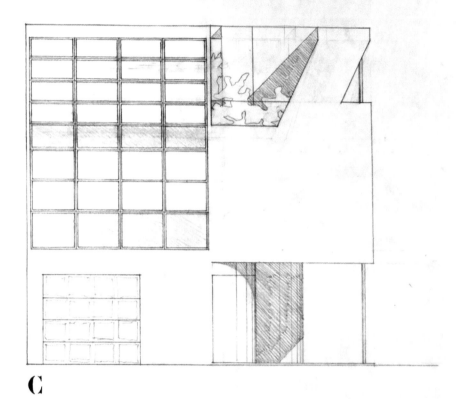

C

4

9'-0"

3

9'-0"

2

9'-0"

1

FILE			
JOB 5	DRAW 2	SCALE 1/4"=1'-0"	
DATE 12-3-30			

A. LAWRENCE KOCHEIOCHE
ALBERT FREY
Architects
4 PARK END PLACE
FOREST HILLS, L. I., N. Y.

EXII. II.

ART. CENTER FOR DARIEN, CONN,
A.L.K. & A.H.

MODEL 1/8" = 1'-0"

Many Kocher and Frey designs were not realized, including this
innovative 1930 design for the Darien Guild Hall in Darien, Connecticut.

SKETCH

Miniature Golf Course (1930)

pencil and ink on paper
ARCHITECTS: A. Lawrence Kocher with Albert Frey
Special Collections, John D. Rockefeller Jr. Library,
The Colonial Williamsburg Foundation
A. Lawrence Kocher Collection, MS 1986.12

54

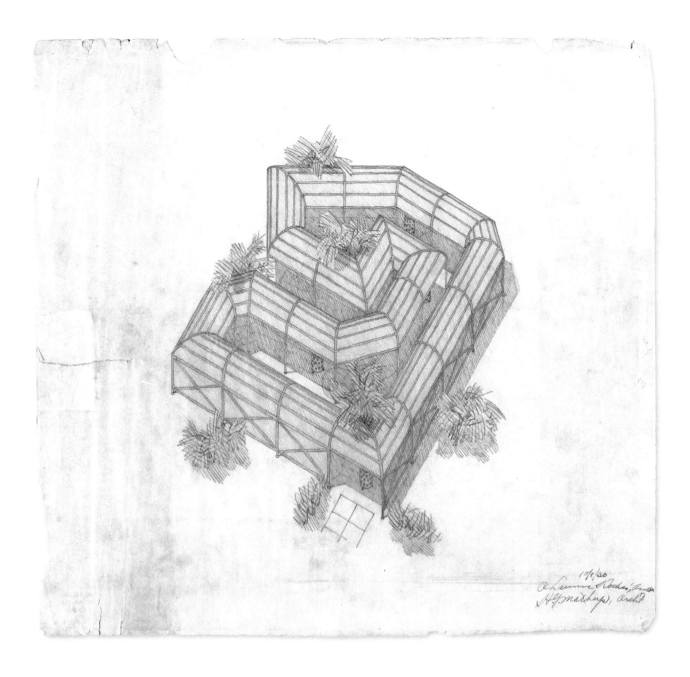

SKETCH

Miniature Golf Course (1930), axonometric view

pencil and ink on paper
ARCHITECTS: A. Lawrence Kocher with Albert Frey
Special Collections, John D. Rockefeller Jr. Library,
The Colonial Williamsburg Foundation
A. Lawrence Kocher Collection, MS 1986.12

MODEL

Farmhouse A (1931)

photographer unknown
ARCHITECTS: A. Lawrence Kocher with Albert Frey
Palm Springs Art Museum
Albert Frey Collection, 55-1999.2, VIIA47-34

following spread:

DRAWING

Ralph-Barbarin House (1932), view from the garden and the street

pencil on paper
ARCHITECTS: A. Lawrence Kocher with Albert Frey
Special Collections, John D. Rockefeller Jr. Library
The Colonial Williamsburg Foundation
A. Lawrence Kocher Collection, MS1986.12

VIEW FROM THE GARDEN

VIEW FROM THE STREET

FILE	G.G , RALPH		
	G. BARBARIN		
JOB 11	DRAW 8		SCALE
DATE APRIL 1932			

A. LAWRENCE KOCHER
ALBERT FREY

4 PARK END PLACE
FOREST HILLS, L. I., N. Y.

Kocher Canvas Week-End House (1934)

photographer unknown
ARCHITECTS: A. Lawrence Kocher and Albert Frey
Palm Springs Art Museum
Jean Farrar Collection
S2020.1, XVB21

60

KEND HOUSE, LONG ISLAND, NEW YORK
R LAWRENCE KOCHER, 1934

FRAMELESS GLASS TABLE

VE1.34

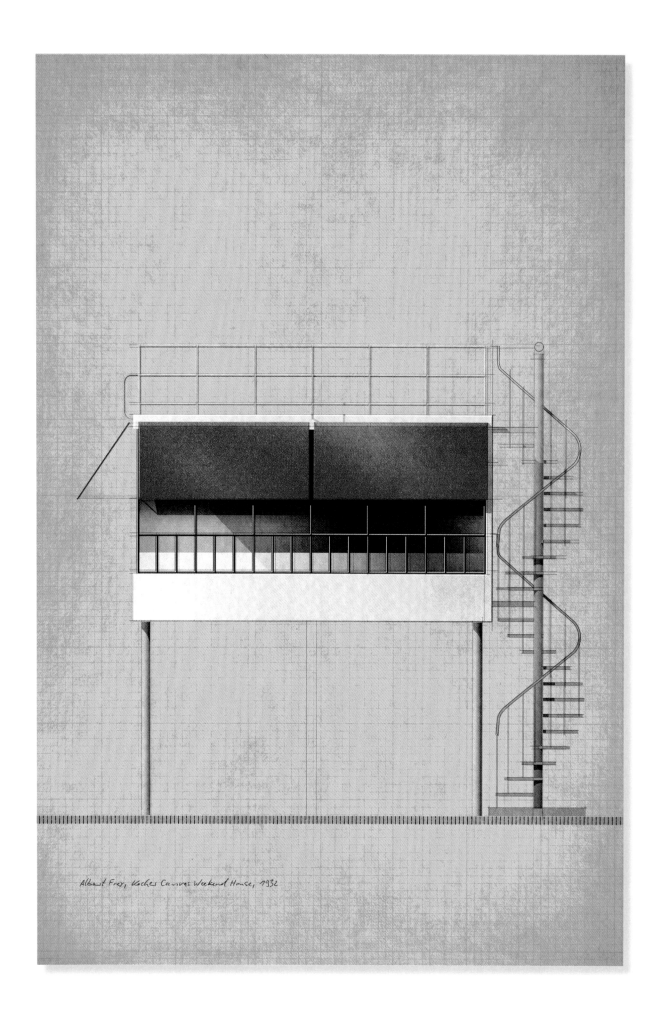

Albert Frey, Koches Canvas Weekend House, 1932

PRINT

Kocher Canvas Week-End House (1934)

by Sander Patelski for Studio Patelski, 2022
ARCHITECTS: A. Lawrence Kocher and Albert Frey
Courtesy of Sander Patelski

Dr. J. J. Kocher was the first full-time doctor in Palm Springs and the brother of New York-based architect A. Lawrence Kocher. Dr. Kocher asked his brother in New York to design a multi-purpose building for him on what is now Palm Canyon Drive, and Frey was the lead designer for the project. Strict, cubist, European modernism found its way to the California desert, metaphorically opening the door for all the modern-style architecture and architects to follow to the small desert outpost.

Albert Frey made the model for the Kocher-Samson building before ever visiting Palm Springs; perhaps he did not know saguaro cactuses were not native to the Palm Springs area.

MODELS

Kocher-Samson Building (1934)

photographed c. 1934, photographer unknown
ARCHITECTS: A. Lawrence Kocher and Albert Frey
Palm Springs Art Museum
Jean Farrar Collection, S2020.1, XVB19

MODEL ¼" = 1'- 0"

A.L.K. & A.F.
DR. J.J. KOCHER   1934-35
OFFICE & APT.
PALM SPRINGS

Kocher-Samson Building (1934) under construction

photographed c. 1934, photographer unknown
ARCHITECTS: A. Lawrence Kocher and Albert Frey
Palm Springs Art Museum
Jean Farrar Collection, S2020.1, XVB20

66

Local photographer Stephen Willard documented the Kocher-Samson building from construction to completion, in daylight and evening, and staged it with the most modern furnishings of its time. Willard's photographs are wholly evocative of the time and place of this important landmark. The building still stands, albeit in dire need of a respectful restoration as of the time of this book's publishing. It is arguably the most important architecture in Palm Springs not restored or rightly celebrated.

This commission would change Albert Frey's life and the history of Palm Springs, as it was the project that brought Frey to the desert.

STEPHEN H. WILLARD

Kocher-Samson Building (1934)

ARCHITECTS: A. Lawrence Kocher and Albert Frey
Palm Springs Art Museum
Albert Frey Collection, 55-1999.2, VIIB45-7

STEPHEN H. WILLARD

Kocher-Samson Building (1934)

ARCHITECTS: A. Lawrence Kocher and Albert Frey
Palm Springs Art Museum
Albert Frey Collection, 55-1999.2, VIIA13-37

STEPHEN H. WILLARD

Kocher-Samson Building (1934)

ARCHITECTS: A. Lawrence Kocher and Albert Frey
Albert Frey papers, Architecture and Design Collection
Art, Design & Architecture Museum
University of California, Santa Barbara

BRANDENSTEIN STUDY · P.S.

VII A 13-3

In 1935, Clark and Frey designed a
modernist house for attorney Henry
U. Brandenstein dubbed "Praeneste."
Albert Frey designed a detached
study for the backyard, seemingly a
precursor to the modern-day accessory
dwelling unit (A.D.U.).

Frey was summoned from Palm Springs to New York City in 1937 to assist architect Philip Goodwin, who was working with Edward Durrell Stone on drawings and concepts for the Museum of Modern Art building on 53rd Street. His main contributions were the details and engineering for the large glass curtain wall at the streetside, an auditorium, a reading room, and, most notably, the large oculi on the roof terrace—the "cheese holes" as one critic proclaimed. Frey would continue to employ circular shapes throughout the rest of his career.

The Museum of Modern Art (1937)

photograph by Albert Frey
ARCHITECTS: Philip L. Goodwin and Edward Durell Stone
Albert Frey papers, Architecture and Design Collection
Art, Design & Architecture Museum
University of California, Santa Barbara

Made almost entirely of cast glass
block with embedded neon for signage,
this round building was meant to glow
like a lantern to attract the attention of
passing motorists.

DRAWING

Dellside Dairy (1939)

pencil on paper
ARCHITECTS: Clark & Frey
Albert Frey papers, Architecture and Design
Collection. Art, Design & Architecture Museum
University of California, Santa Barbara

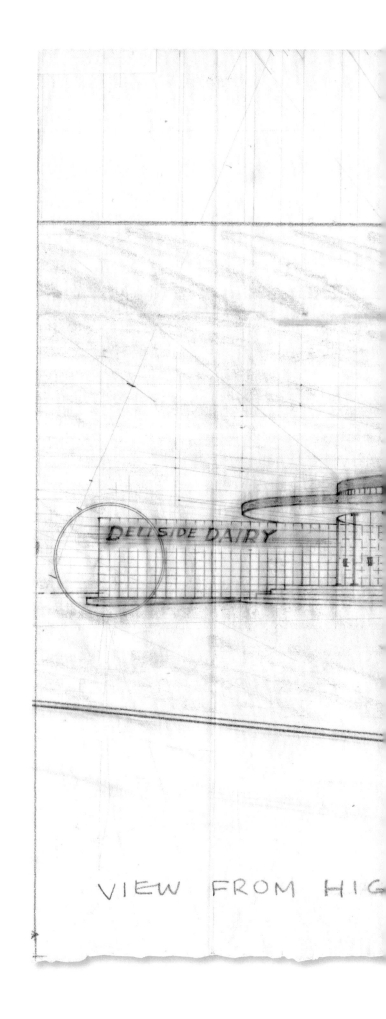

DELLSIDE DAIRY

VIEW FROM HIG

DELLSIDE
DAIRY

AY

IN SEARCH

BY ALBERT FREY
ARCHITECTURAL BOOK
PUBLISHING CO., INC.
NEW YORK

OF A

LIVING

ARCHITECT

In 1939, Frey published a small book, *In Search of a Living Architecture*, stating his philosophy and ideals with illustrations of some of his earliest architectural work, designs by other influential architects, and snapshots he took—inspired by agricultural and industrial vernacular designs and buildings—on his first American cross-country road trip.

ALBERT FREY

In Search of Living Architecture, original edition, 1939

Palm Springs Art Museum
Jean Farrar Collection, S2020.1, XVC10

In 1938, Albert married writer Marion
Cook in New York, and she moved to Palm
Springs with him. They lived a life of relative
domestic bliss in a rental home (the Mason
Duplex designed by Clark & Frey, 1937)
before Albert designed and built their first
house.The marriage did not last; Cook
missed New York and did not want to live
in Palm Springs. They divorced in 1945.
Neither remarried but remained friends
and pen pals for the rest of their lives. The
couple would travel extensively during the
short time they were together. These rare
photos showing Marion were taken at the
Grand Canyon in 1939.

Frey photos from the Grand Canyon, 1939

GRAND CANYON, ARIZONA 1939

Until his death, Frey would show visitors and students these simple illustrations that distilled his principles of architecture to their most basic forms.

ALBERT FREY

Elements of Building Spaces: 5. Composition, 1940

pencil on paper
Palm Springs Art Museum
Albert Frey Collection, 55-1999.2, VC40-1

following spread:

Elements of Building Spaces: 1. Floor Slab, 1940
Elements of Building Spaces: 2. Wall Unit, 1940
Elements of Building Spaces: 3. Glass Unit, 1940
Elements of Building Spaces: 4. Roof Unit, 1940

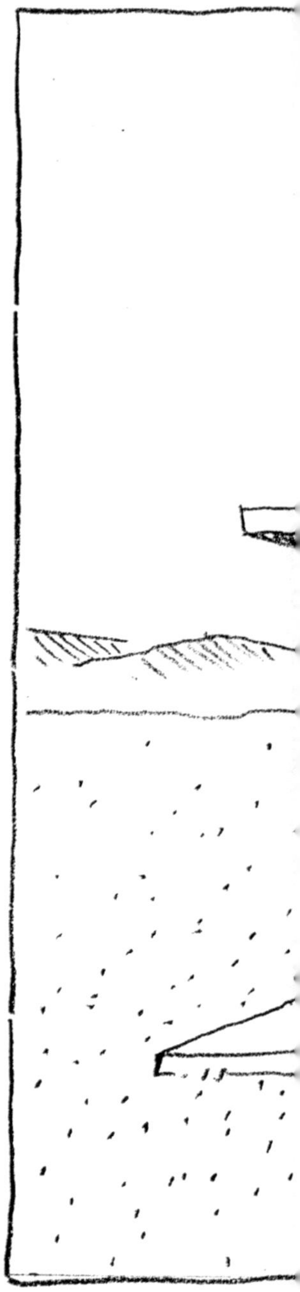

5. COM

SITION

Albert Frey
1940-90

ALBERT FREY, ARCHITECT
686 PALISADES DRIVE FAIA
PALM SPRINGS, CALIFORNIA 92262

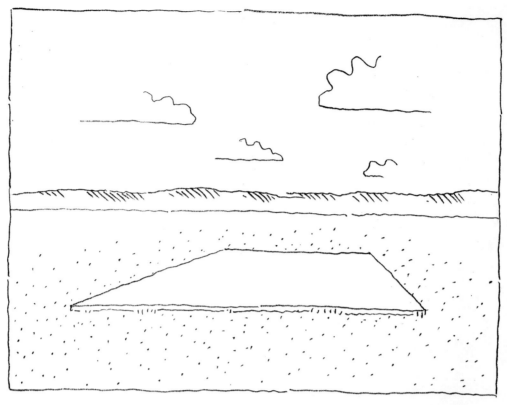

1. FLOOR SLAB

2. WALL UNIT

3. GLASS UNIT

Albert Frey
1940-90

ALBERT FREY, ARCHITECT
686 PALISADES DRIVE FAIA
PALM SPRINGS, CALIFORNIA 92262

4. ROOF UNIT

Albert Frey
1940-90

ALBERT FREY, ARCHITECT
686 PALISADES DRIVE FAIA
PALM SPRINGS, CALIFORNIA 92262

JOHN PORTER CLARK & ALBERT FREY

Sun Chart - Palm Springs, 1935

ink and pencil on paper
Palm Springs Art Museum
Albert Frey Collection, 55-1999.2, VIIIL14

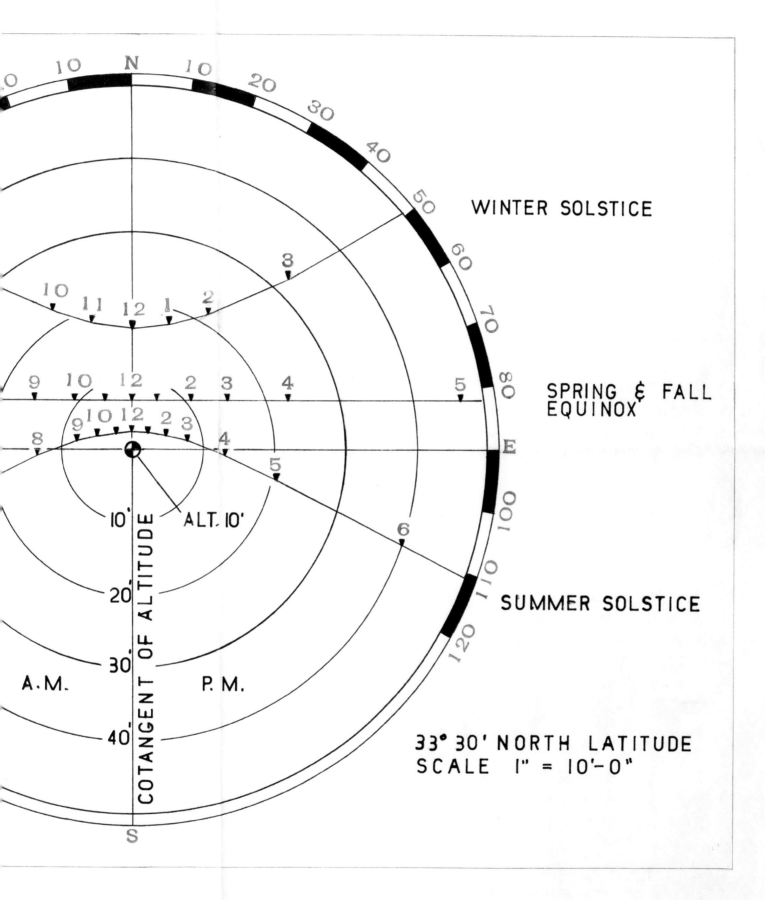

WINTER SOLSTICE

SPRING & FALL
EQUINOX

SUMMER SOLSTICE

33° 30' NORTH LATITUDE
SCALE 1" = 10'-0"

ALT. 10'

COTANGENT OF ALTITUDE

A.M.   P.M.

ᵗᵏ & ALBERT FREY   SUNCHART — PALM SPRINGS

Frey fell in love with Palm Springs soon after he arrived in 1934 to supervise construction of the Kocher-Samson Building. Deciding to make Palm Springs home in 1940, Frey was finally able to design and build his first Palm Springs house for himself and his new wife, Marion Cook, a writer, and it was an avant-garde revelation. This shockingly modern and unusual home alone in the wild desert was a beautiful juxtaposition. Frey's two-acre property was part of a larger parcel that would eventually feature homes by E. Stewart Williams, John Porter Clark, and Culver Nichols near the corner of what is now Via Donna and Paseo El Mirador in Palm Springs. The first incarnation was very small in size (basically one room, approximately 320 square feet), but Frey would constantly add on to and change the structure over the years, using the house as his personal laboratory to explore and expand on his ideas and test new materials.

Frey House I (1940)

photographer unknown
ARCHITECTS: Clark & Frey
Palm Springs Art Museum
Jean Farrar Collection, S2020.1, XVB14

JULIUS SHULMAN

Frey House I (1940)

photographed 1947
ARCHITECTS: Clark & Frey
Getty Research Institute, Los Angeles
(2004.R.10). © J. Paul Getty Trust.

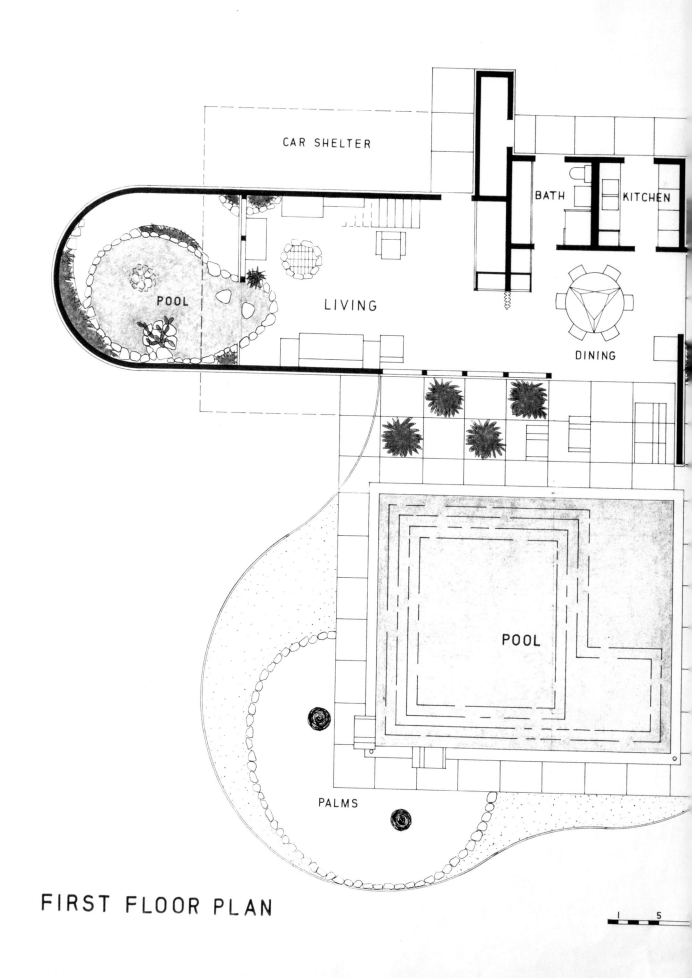

CAR SHELTER

BATH   KITCHEN

POOL

LIVING

DINING

POOL

PALMS

FIRST FLOOR PLAN

1   5

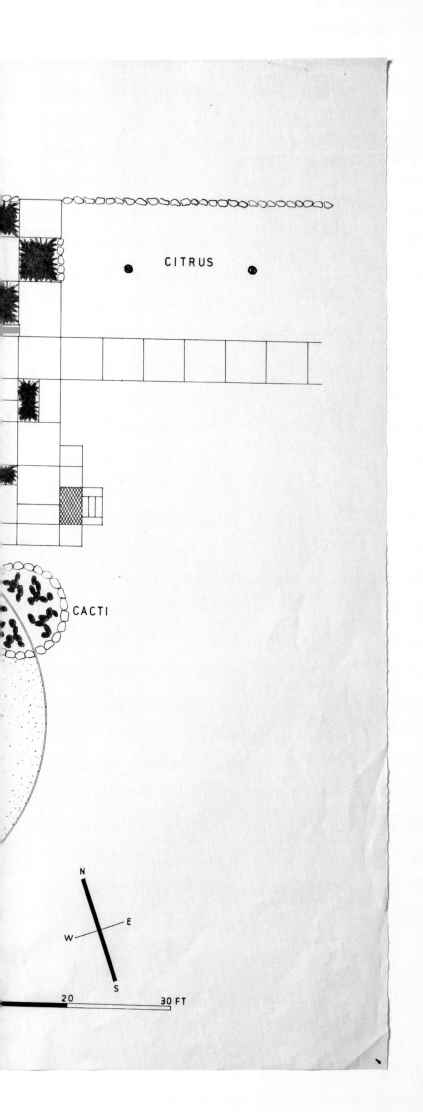

CITRUS

CACTI

N

E

W

S

20   30 FT

DRAWING

Frey House I (1940) with additions c. 1953

ARCHITECTS: Clark & Frey
Palm Springs Art Museum
Albert Frey Collection, 55-1999.2, VIIIC4

THE HOUSE overlooks a garden-side pool

M. THATCHER

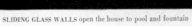

SLIDING GLASS WALLS open the house to pool and fountain

A large viewpoint will increase the apparent size of a house. The visibility of Mr. Frey's house in Palm Springs is not limited to its tiny size (16' x 20'). Nearly half of the walls are of sliding glass. From two corners of the living area (see sketch, *left*) large, fin-like walls extend into the landscape to define two terraces; together with the projecting planes of floor and ceiling, they add to the visual square footage. One wall, a warm rose color, forms a solid background to the room; the other, a pale receding green, blends into the atmosphere and the desert colors.

The 1948 remodel to Frey House I added a larger living room and sleeping area with a small, indoor/outdoor water feature, a more organic version of what had been done with the swimming pool at the Loewy House (1946). A fireplace and skylight were also added. From his bed, Frey had elements of nature—fire, water, and sky—in close proximity. The last thing he could see before falling asleep was the cosmos.

JULIUS SHULMAN

Frey House I (1940) interior

photographed c. 1950
ARCHITECTS: Clark & Frey
Getty Research Institute, Los Angeles
(2004.R.10). © J. Paul Getty Trust

In 1953, Frey added a second-story bedroom, accessed by a suspended staircase, that became known as the "Flash Gordon suite" for its sci-fi futuristic appearance. Frey would later use a similar staircase design at the North Shore Yacht Club (1958).

JULIUS SHULMAN

Frey House I (1940) interior

photographed 1954, 1956
ARCHITECTS: Clark & Frey
Getty Research Institute, Los Angeles
(2004.R.10). © J. Paul Getty Trust.

Frey and Austin-Healey in front of Frey House I (1940)

photographed in 1953
photographer unknown
ARCHITECTS: Clark & Frey
Palm Springs Art Museum
Jean Farrar Collection, S2020.1, XVB14

JULIUS SHULMAN

Frey House I (1940) with addition

photographed 1954, 1956
ARCHITECTS: Clark & Frey
Getty Research Institute, Los Angeles
(2004.R.10). © J. Paul Getty Trust

Frey House I (1940) with addition

photographed c. 1960s
photographer unknown
ARCHITECTS: Clark & Frey
Image #146-10644 © *Palm Springs Life* archives
Palm Springs Historical Society

JULIUS SHULMAN

Frey House I (1940) with addition

photographed 1954, 1956
ARCHITECTS: Clark & Frey
Palm Springs Art Museum
Museum Purchase, 29-2007.3
Getty Research Institute, Los Angeles
(2004.R.10). © J. Paul Getty Trust

JULIUS SHULMAN

Frey House I (1940)

photographed 1954, 1956
ARCHITECTS: Clark & Frey
Getty Research Institute, Los Angeles
(2004.R.10). © J. Paul Getty Trust

In the mid-1940s, Frey designed and built a small guest house on his property. Richard Neutra stayed there while overseeing construction of his Kaufmann House (1946). Photographer and friend Julius Shulman was also a frequent guest.

Two of Frey's most significant early desert designs of the 1940s were the Hatton House (1945) and the Loewy House (1946), similar ideas on geologically different sites. Hatton's house was situated on flat open land, now Rancho Mirage, while Raymond Loewy's house (dubbed "Tierra Caliente") is next door to Richard Neutra's Kaufmann House (1947) in Palm Springs, on a gentle slope, set among large boulders spilling down from Chino Canyon. Both houses are simple in rectilinear form with flat roofs and walls that extend out from the house itself onto the landscape, creating visual structural stability and horizontal expansiveness. Both featured what became a signature Frey material— corrugated metal panels for walls.

Frey wanted to blur the boundaries the between interior and exterior
space, as exemplified by the swimming pool at Loewy House that meandered
under a large retractable glass wall and into the living room.
He would copy this gesture with a small water feature at his own home,
Frey House I, when he remodeled it in 1948.

SHULMAN

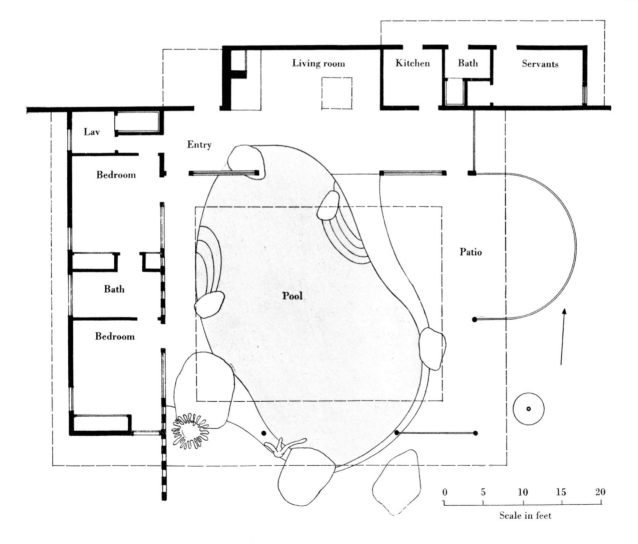

Living room   Kitchen   Bath   Servants

Lav

Entry

Bedroom

Patio

Bath

Pool

Bedroom

0   5   10   15   20

Scale in feet

JULIUS SHULMAN

Loewy House (1946)

photographed 1947
ARCHITECTS: Clark & Frey with Raymond Loewy
Getty Research Institute, Los Angeles
(2004.R.10). © J. Paul Getty Trust

JULIUS SHULMAN

Clark & Frey Building (1947)

photographed 1950
ARCHITECTS: Clark & Frey
Getty Research Institute, Los Angeles
(2004.R.10). © J. Paul Getty Trust

JULIUS SHULMAN

Clark & Frey Building (1947)

photographed 1950
ARCHITECTS: Clark & Frey
Palm Springs Art Museum
Museum purchase, 29-2007.27
Getty Research Institute, Los Angeles
(2004.R.10). © J. Paul Getty Trust

DRAWING

Paddock Pool Company Building (1947)

ARCHITECTS: Clark & Frey
Albert Frey papers, Architecture and Design
Collection. Art, Design & Architecture Museum
University of California, Santa Barbara

Film star and Frey client Raymond Hatton donned his cowboy
garb and posed for publicity photos at the Desert Bank, the first
drive-up bank in the Coachella Valley.

JULIUS SHULMAN

Palm Springs City Hall (1952–1957)

photographed 1958
ARCHITECTS: Clark, Frey & Chambers;
Williams, Williams, and Williams
Getty Research Institute, Los Angeles
(2004.R.10). © J. Paul Getty Trust

122

Frey had previously designed the Desert Hills Hotel on this site for local developer Tony Burke—a project that fell through prior to construction. Raymond Cree bought the property and also developed a similar scheme for multiple homes, though only one was ever built, which he occupied. The structure was built with almost all industrial materials and clad in a favorite siding of Frey's at the time— asbestos-impregnated cement board stamped with a wood grain pattern. The color was integral; it never required painting and was fireproof and mold proof, reflecting Frey's lifelong interest in low-maintenance construction and longevity. These materials, along with the yellow corrugated fiberglass panels inspired by Encelia flowers and a dramatic chimney in natural rock from the site, make an assertive and impressive statement.

JULIUS SHULMAN

Hill House [Cree II] (1955)

photographed 1957
ARCHITECTS: Clark, Frey & Chambers
Getty Research Institute, Los Angeles
(2004.R.10). © J. Paul Getty Trust

The design for the Premiere Apartments (1957) was perhaps the most exuberant and playful of all of Frey's work. Multicolored fiber-glass panels created privacy zones, embossed diamond-patterned aluminum panels clad the exterior, his signature ergonomic concrete seating flanked the amoebic shaped biomorphic pool, and metal porthole windows cut on a bias capped each end. When Frey learned of its possible destruction, he helped coordinate its move, one block away, saving it. It survived until a fire destroyed it in 2007. Like Hill House [Cree II], the Premiere Apartments reflect Frey's choice of innovative construction materials and his bold expressionistic artistry.

JULIUS SHULMAN

North Shore Yacht Club (1958)

photographed 1960
ARCHITECTS: Frey & Chambers
Palm Springs Art Museum
Museum purchase, 29-2007.39
Getty Research Institute, Los Angeles
(2004.R.10). © J. Paul Getty Trust

Saint Michael's By-The-Sea Episcopal Church (1958) is one of Frey's most artistic compositions in concrete block. As in his other concrete-block creations, Frey would have the block lightly sandblasted to give it a more organic, weathered appearance, exposing the intricate colors of the aggregate. The openings in the block were infilled with stained glass, mainly shades of green on the sides and radiating gradations of purples and lavenders above the altar.

following spread:

DRAWING

American Red Cross Riverside County Chapter House (1959)

RED CROSS BLDG. RIVERSIDE, CA

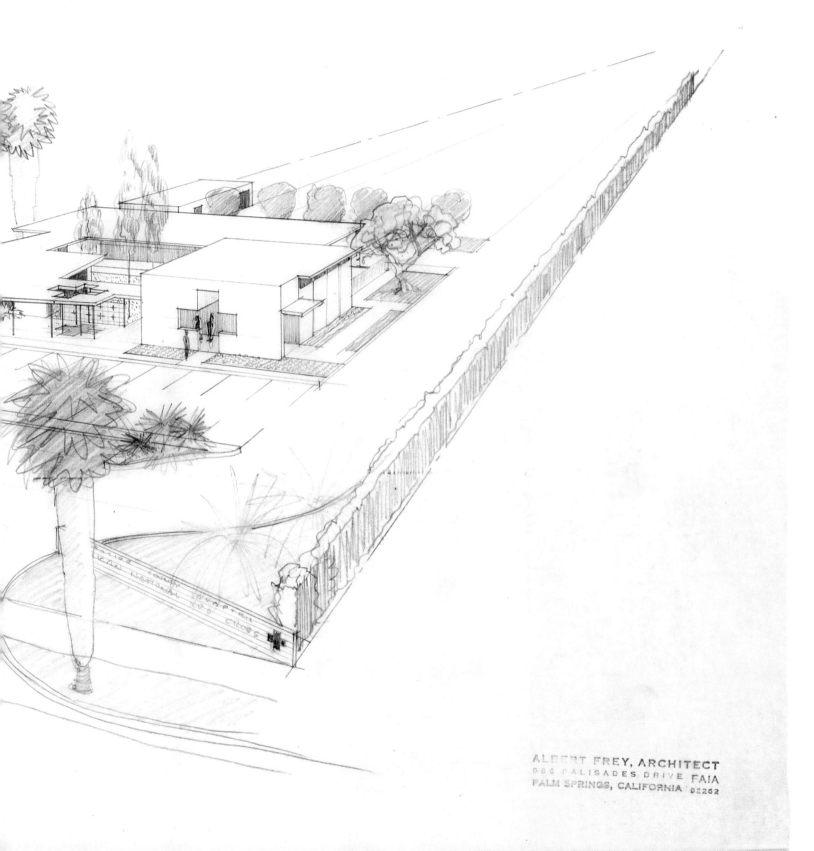

ALBERT FREY, ARCHITECT
686 PALISADES DRIVE FAIA
PALM SPRINGS, CALIFORNIA 92262

TROPICAL FOLIAGE
8-1-59   WAIKIKI

ALBERT FREY

Tropical Foliage, 1959

colored pencil on paper
Palm Springs Art Museum
Albert Frey Collection 55-1999.2, IVA30

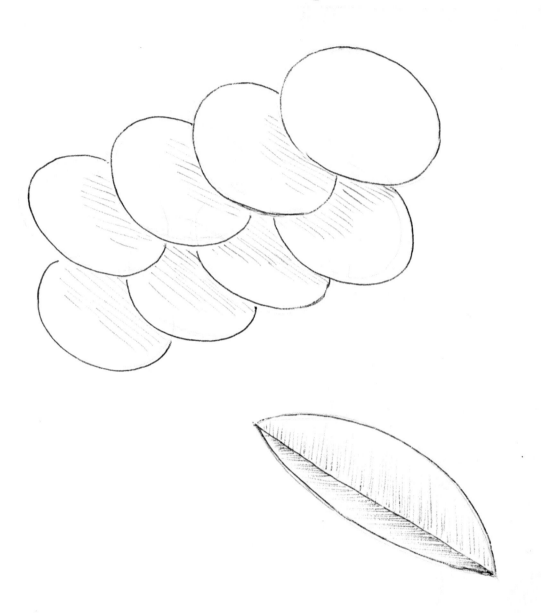

ABSTRACTED LEAVE SHAPES
SUITABLE FOR SHEET METAL FORMING
7-30-59

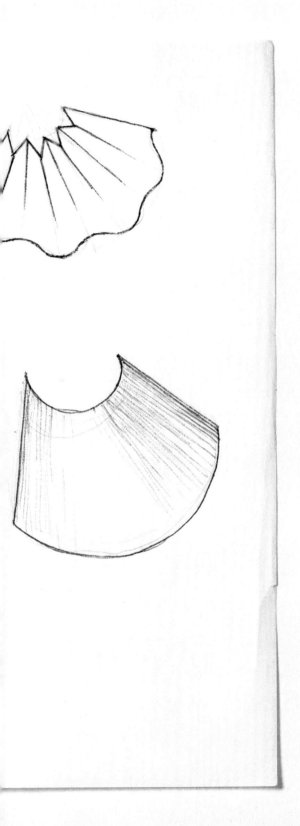

opposite:

ALBERT FREY

*Abstracted Leave Shapes Suitable
for Sheet Metal Forming*, 1959

pencil on paper
Palm Springs Art Museum
Albert Frey Collection 55-1999.2, IVA30

Frey designed many projects for friend
and developer Culver Nichols, including this
shopping center—with a geodesic-domed
restaurant as its centerpiece—on a property
adjacent to Nichols's Tramway Gas Station (1965).
The center was never built.

following spread:

DRAWING

Nichols Neighborhood Shopping Center (1962)

ARCHITECTS: Frey & Chambers
Albert Frey papers, Architecture and Design Collection
Art, Design & Architecture Museum
University of California, Santa Barbara

TRAM WAY

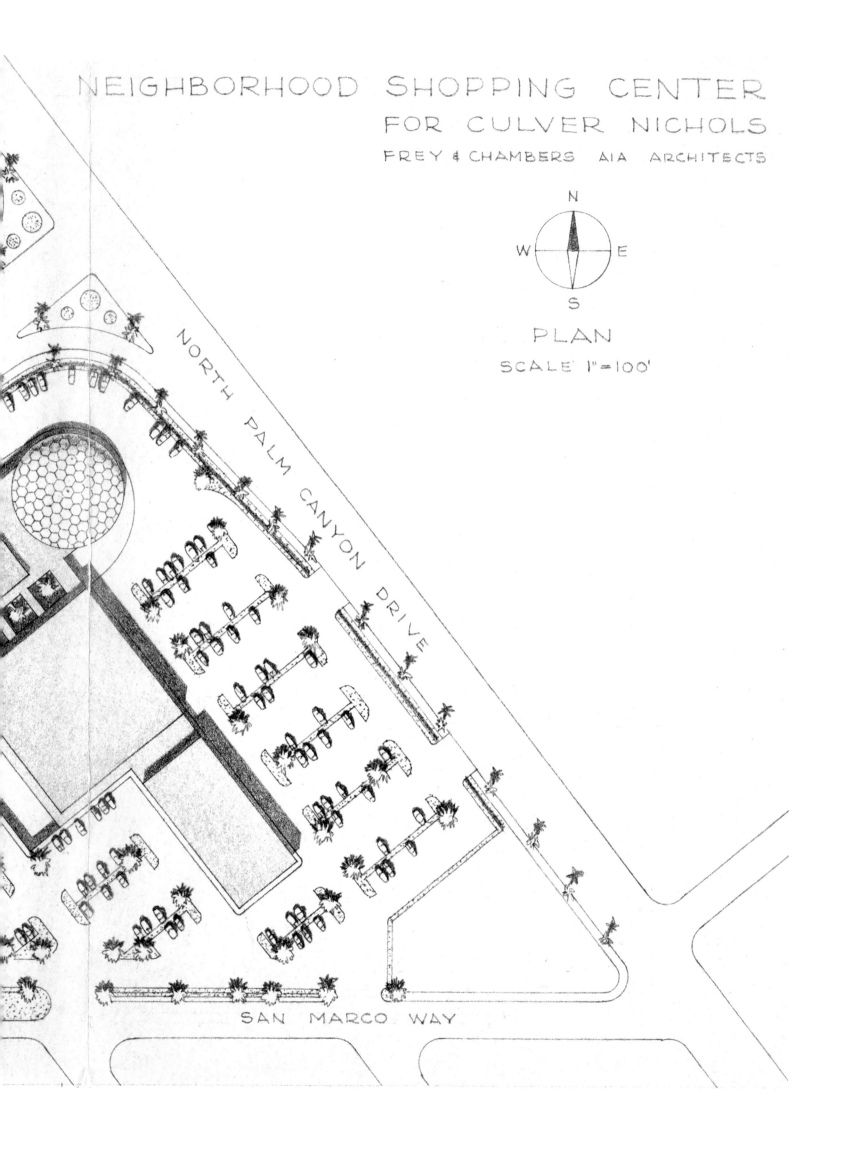

NEIGHBORHOOD SHOPPING CENTER
FOR CULVER NICHOLS
FREY & CHAMBERS AIA ARCHITECTS

N
W · E
S

PLAN
SCALE 1"=100'

NORTH PALM CANYON DRIVE

SAN MARCO WAY

Inspired visually by East Coast covered bridges, Frey's innovative design for the Aerial Tramway Valley Station (1949–1963) would allow occasional severe storm debris and dangerous runoff from the mountain to pass safely under the structure. The roof line mimics the slope of the rocks and mountain, and its walls are, in part, exposed structural trusses that, when infilled with glass, create a dramatic picture window showcasing the drama of the tram and its cabled path up to the San Jacinto Peak and the mountain station designed by E. Stewart Williams (8,516 feet above sea level). Visitors are carried from the desert to an alpine forest environment in approximately ten minutes.

Palm Springs Aerial Tramway Valley Station (1949–1963)

photographer unknown
ARCHITECTS: Williams, Clark, Frey & Chambers
Courtesy of the *Los Angeles Herald Examiner* Photo Collection
Los Angeles Public Library

following spread:

JULIUS SHULMAN

Palm Springs Aerial Tramway Valley Station (1949–1963)

photographed 1964
ARCHITECTS: Williams, Clark, Frey & Chambers
Getty Research Institute, Los Angeles
(2004.R.10). © J. Paul Getty Trust

Frey House II (1963)—the project where his lifelong studies of materiality, sustainability, composition, and sensitivity to site and color all came together— is arguably Frey's masterpiece.

After living on the desert floor for decades and looking up at the hills, he thought "it might be nice to live up there." He searched for an inspiring site for five years and purchased—for approximately $30,000—what was deemed to be an "unbuildable lot" 220 feet above the desert floor.

The roof plane is the main sculptural element, as the house is essentially a giant sunshade propped up on a large boulder enclosed with walls of glass.

JULIUS SHULMAN

Frey House II (1963)

photographed 1965
ARCHITECT: Albert Frey
Getty Research Institute, Los Angeles
(2004.R.10). © J. Paul Getty Trust

following gatefold:

DRAWINGS

Frey House II (1963)

ARCHITECT: Albert Frey
Palm Springs Art Museum
Albert Frey Collection 55-1999.2, VIIIC5

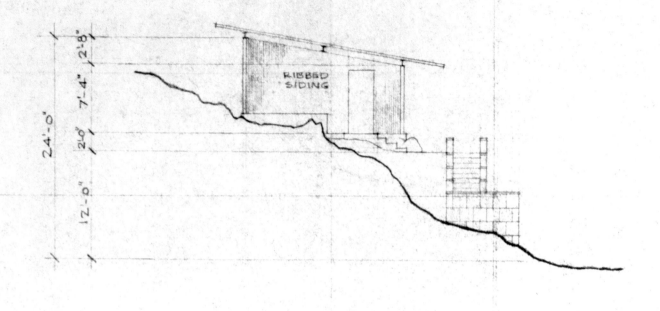

RIBBED
SIDING

24'-0" 12'-0" 2'-0" 7'-4" 2'-8"

WEST

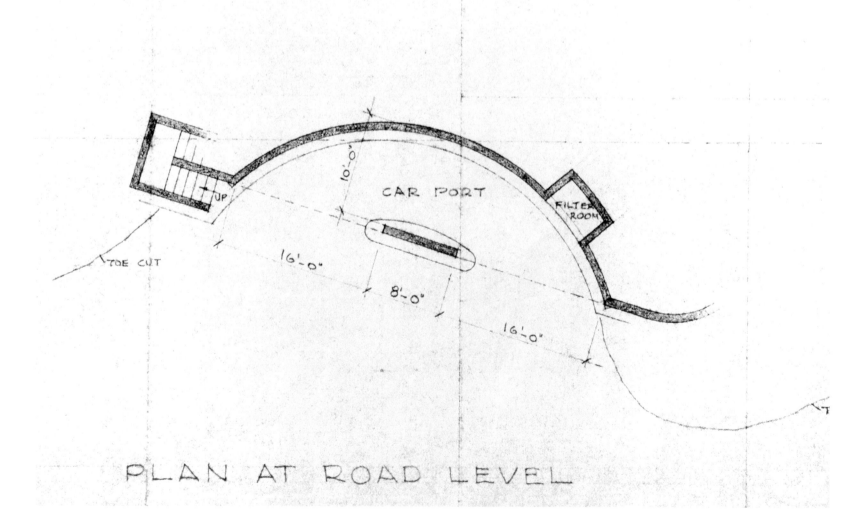

UP

TOE CUT

16'-0"

10'-0"

CAR PORT

8'-0"

FILTER
ROOM

16'-0"

PLAN AT ROAD LEVEL

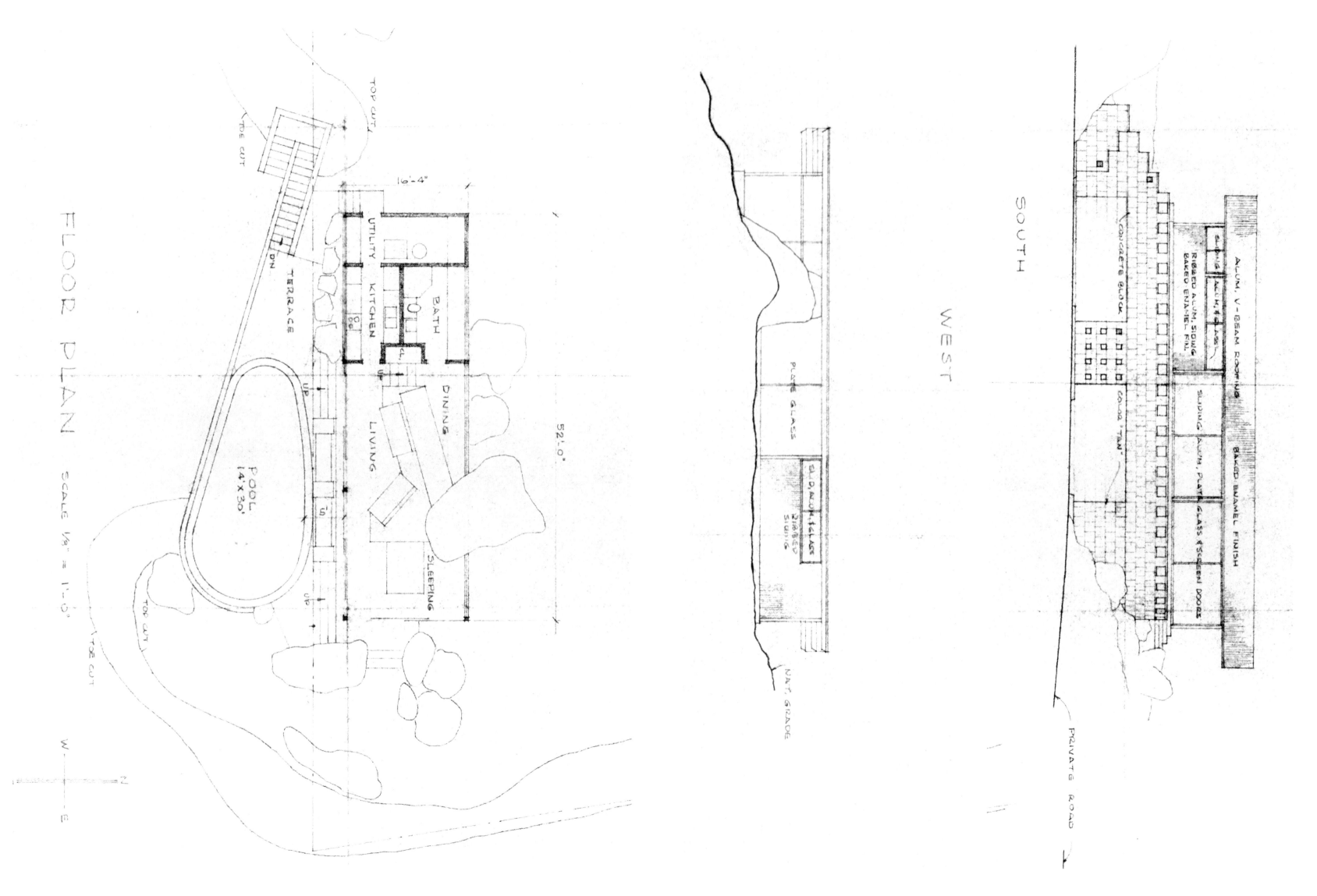

FLOOR PLAN SCALE 1/8" = 1'-0"

POOL 14' X 30'

TERRACE

UTILITY   KITCHEN

BATH

DINING

LIVING

SLEEPING

16'-4"

52'-0"

TOP CUT

TOE CUT

DN

UP

UP

UP

CL.

TOP CUT

TOE CUT

WEST

SOUTH

PLATE GLASS

RIBBED GLASS SIDING

NAT. GRADE

ALUM. V-BEAM ROOFING

RIBBED ALUM. SIDING
BAKED ENAMEL FIN.

SLIDING ALUM. PLATE GLASS # SCREEN DOORS

BAKED ENAMEL FINISH

CONCRETE BLOCK

CO-OP "TAN"

SLIDING ALUM. + GLASS

PRIVATE ROAD

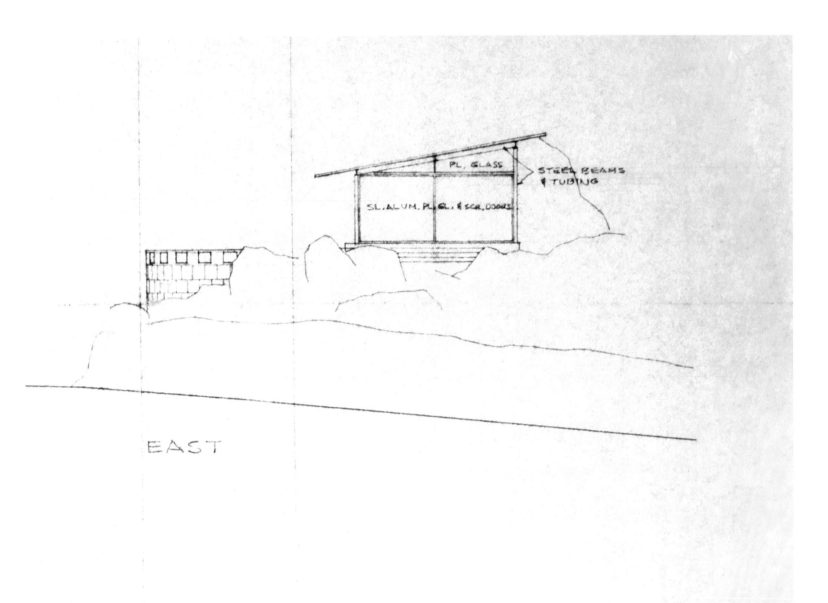

EAST

PRELIMINARY
SITE & FLOOR PLANS,
ELEVATIONS

HOUSE FOR
ALBERT FREY

PALM SPRINGS
PALISADES

FREY & CHAMBERS, ARCHITECTS
878 NORTH PALM CANYON DRIVE
PALM SPRINGS, CALIFORNIA AIA

INDEX 6315
DATE 8-22-63
REVISED 9-6-63

DRAWN BY AF
CHECKED BY

PR 1

NO. 2

PL. GLASS
STEEL BEAMS & TUBING
SL. ALUM. PL. GL. & SCR. DOORS

JULIUS SHULMAN

Frey House II (1963)

photographed 1965
ARCHITECT: Albert Frey
Getty Research Institute, Los Angeles
(2004.R.10). © J. Paul Getty Trust

To have a giant boulder situated in one's house, right next to one's bed, one must really love nature, and this dramatic gesture reflects Frey's commitment to integrating architecture and nature in daring and innovative ways. Frey lived out the rest of his life here—surrounded by sunrises, sunsets, and panoramic vistas—feeding the animals he befriended and welcoming guests and pilgrims.

JULIUS SHULMAN

Frey House II (1963)

photographed 1965
ARCHITECT: Albert Frey
Getty Research Institute, Los Angeles
(2004.R.10). © J. Paul Getty Trust

following spread:

LANCE GERBER

Frey House II (1963)

photographed 2023
ARCHITECT: Albert Frey
Courtesy of *Palm Springs Life*

In 1972, Frey added an extension to Frey House II, a back bedroom that enlarged the house to approximately 1,220 square feet. Frey died on November 14, 1998, in that back bedroom. His modest pink granite grave marker is at the far northwestern corner of nearby Welwood Murray Cemetery.

DRAWING

Frey House II addition (1972)

pen and pencil on paper
ARCHITECT: Albert Frey
Palm Springs Art Museum
Albert Frey Collection 55-1999.2, VIIIC5

following spread:

LANCE GERBER

Frey House II (1963)

photographed 2023
ARCHITECT: Albert Frey
Courtesy of *Palm Springs Life*

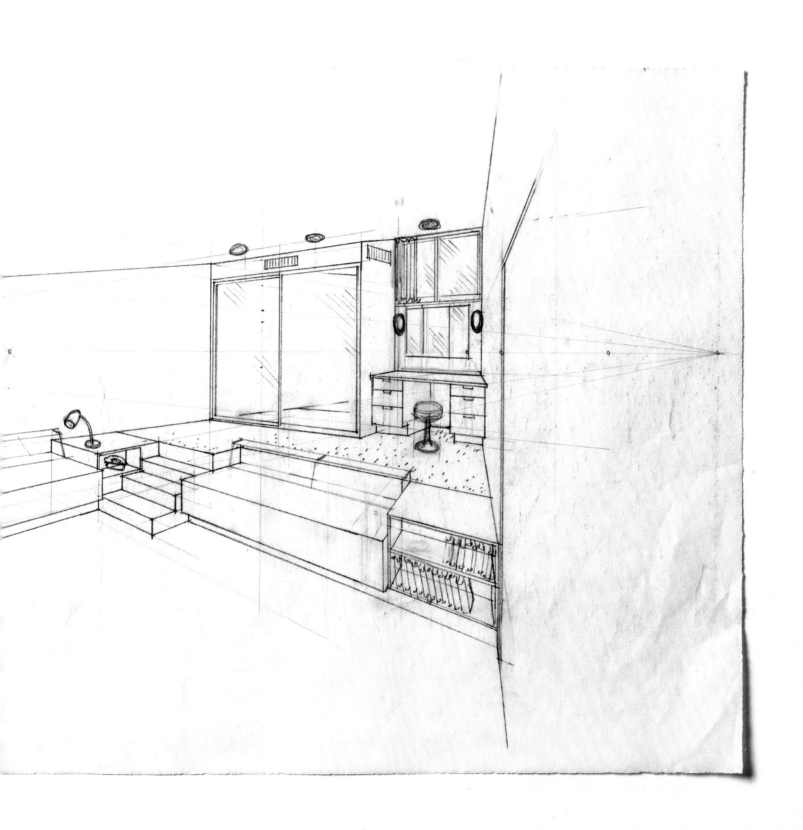

Details of the curtains, Swiss bell, siding,
and clock at Frey House II (1963)

photographed 2023
ARCHITECT: Albert Frey
Courtesy of Radius Books

"When you think what nature produces in fantastic forms, in birds and animals and everything. That's where creativity comes in."

— ALBERT FREY TO JENNIFER GOLUB

Albert Frey / Houses 1+2 (New York: Princeton Architectural Press, 1999), 77.

At the same location where, some twenty-three years earlier, Clark & Frey designed the graceful stone entry gates to Palm Springs, another Frey welcome mat was created. What is now known as the Tramway Gas Station (1965) was to be a bold and assertive monument—architecturally speaking, a hyperbolic paraboloid with a ninety-five-foot wingspan roof—and a symbol that visitors were entering a decidedly mid-century modern, forward-thinking city.

In 1996, the building was approved by the city for demolition, sparking the beginning of the mid-century preservation movement in Palms Springs. The building was saved by those who bravely stood up for its artistry, its physical representation of a moment in time and place, and the legacy of Albert Frey. By divine accident, Frey's designs now greet visitors at the north entrance (Tramway Gas Station), east end (City Hall, for those arriving at the airport) and south end at Highway III (Cree House II) of Palm Springs.

DRAWING

Nichols Service Station [Tramway Gas Station] (1965)

pencil on paper
ARCHITECTS: Frey & Chambers
Albert Frey papers, Architecture and Design Collection
Art, Design & Architecture Museum
University of California, Santa Barbara

CULVER NICHOLS   PALM SPRINGS   FREY & CHAMBERS, ARCHITECTS A.I.A.

BILL ANDERSON

Nichols Service Station
[Tramway Gas Station] (1965)

photographed c. 1968
ARCHITECTS: Frey & Chambers
Collection of Palm Springs Art Museum
Gift of Mrs. Dorothy M. Anderson

DRAWING

Nichols Service Station [Tramway Gas Station] (1965)

pen on paper
ARCHITECTS: Frey & Chambers
Palm Springs Art Museum
Albert Frey Collection, 55-1999.2, VIIIG1

1 GASOLINE PUMPS
2 SALES ROOM & OFF
3 LUBE & WASH BAY
4 STORAGE
5 TOILETS
6 PARKING
7 FOUNTAIN & POO

TRAMWAY

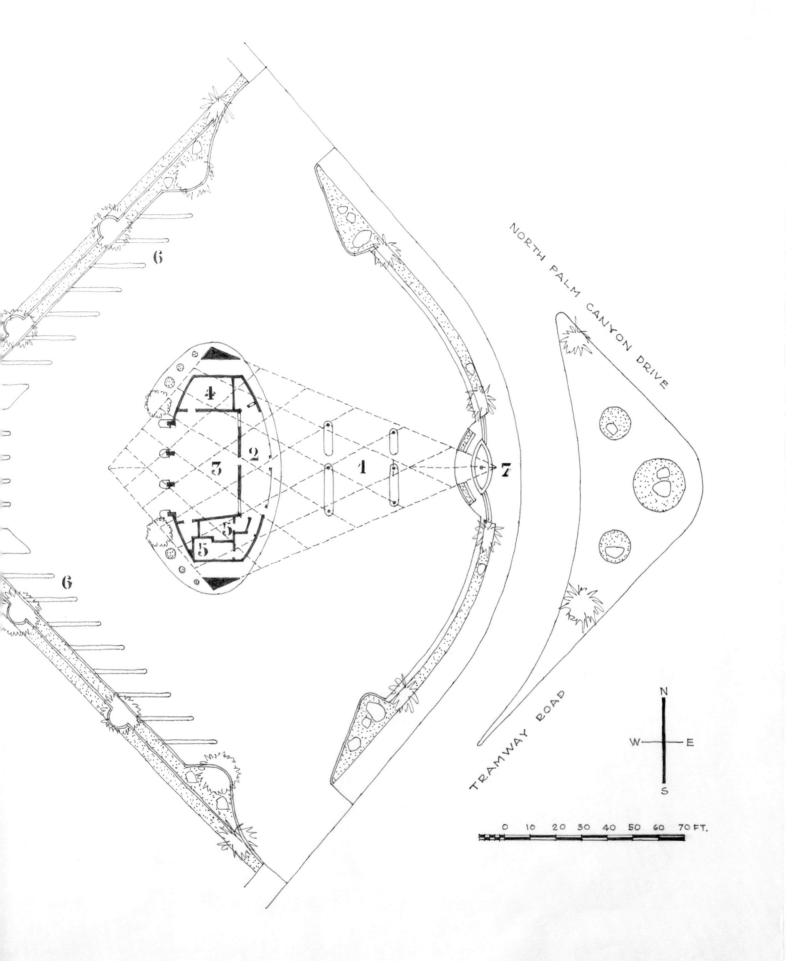

6

6

4

2

3

5

5

1

7

NORTH PALM CANYON DRIVE

TRAMWAY ROAD

N
W — E
S

0   10   20   30   40   50   60   70 FT.

VICE STATION — SITE & FLOOR PLAN —

PALM SPRINGS, CALIFORNIA 92262
FREY & CHAMBERS, ARCHITECTS, AIA

DRAWING

Shell Oil Company Service Station (1965)

ARCHITECTS: Frey & Chambers
Palm Springs Art Museum
Albert Frey Collection, 55-1999.2, VIIC27-2

following spread:

DRAWING

Store Building No. 2
for Culver Nichols (1968)

pen on paper
ARCHITECT: Albert Frey
Albert Frey papers, Architecture and Design
Collection. Art, Design & Architecture Museum
University of California, Santa Barbara

VIEW FROM PALM CANYON D

STORE NO. 2
NICHOLS
ALBERT FREY. FAIA
1-2-69   681

Vacation Cottage (1997) was the last house Frey was commissioned to design. Never built, the small residence was designed for any climate—polar, temperate, arid, or tropical.

On his first road trip across America, Frey photographed grain silo roof domes that he admired. He had wanted to use this element on a residence his entire career and, decades later, found the right project.

DRAWING

Vacation Cottage (1997)

pencil on paper
ARCHITECT: Albert Frey
Private collection

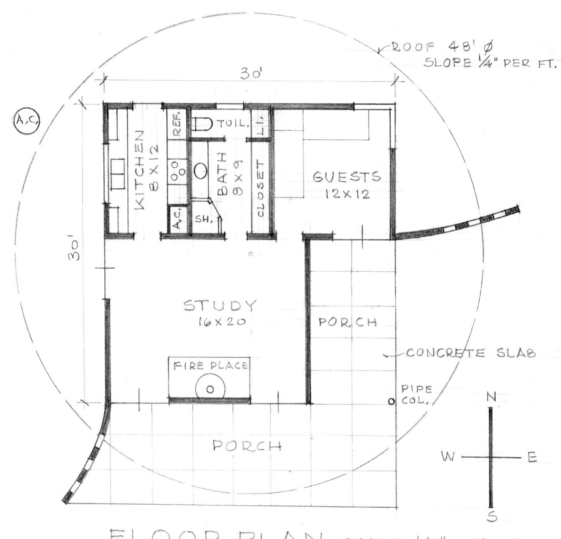

METAL EDGE   COMPO ROOFING

8'

CONCRETE BLOCK   SLIDING DOORS

SOUTH ELEVATION

ROOF 48' ⌀
SLOPE ¼" PER FT.

30'

(A,C)

30'

KITCHEN 8×12

REF.   TOIL.   LI.

BATH 8×9

CLOSET

A.C.   SH.

GUESTS 12×12

STUDY 16×20

PORCH

FIRE PLACE

CONCRETE SLAB

PIPE COL.

PORCH

N
W   E
S

ALBERT FREY, ARCHITECT FAIA

FLOOR PLAN SCALE 1/8" = 1'-0"

BD-TF-JM COTTAGE DATE: 2-4-97

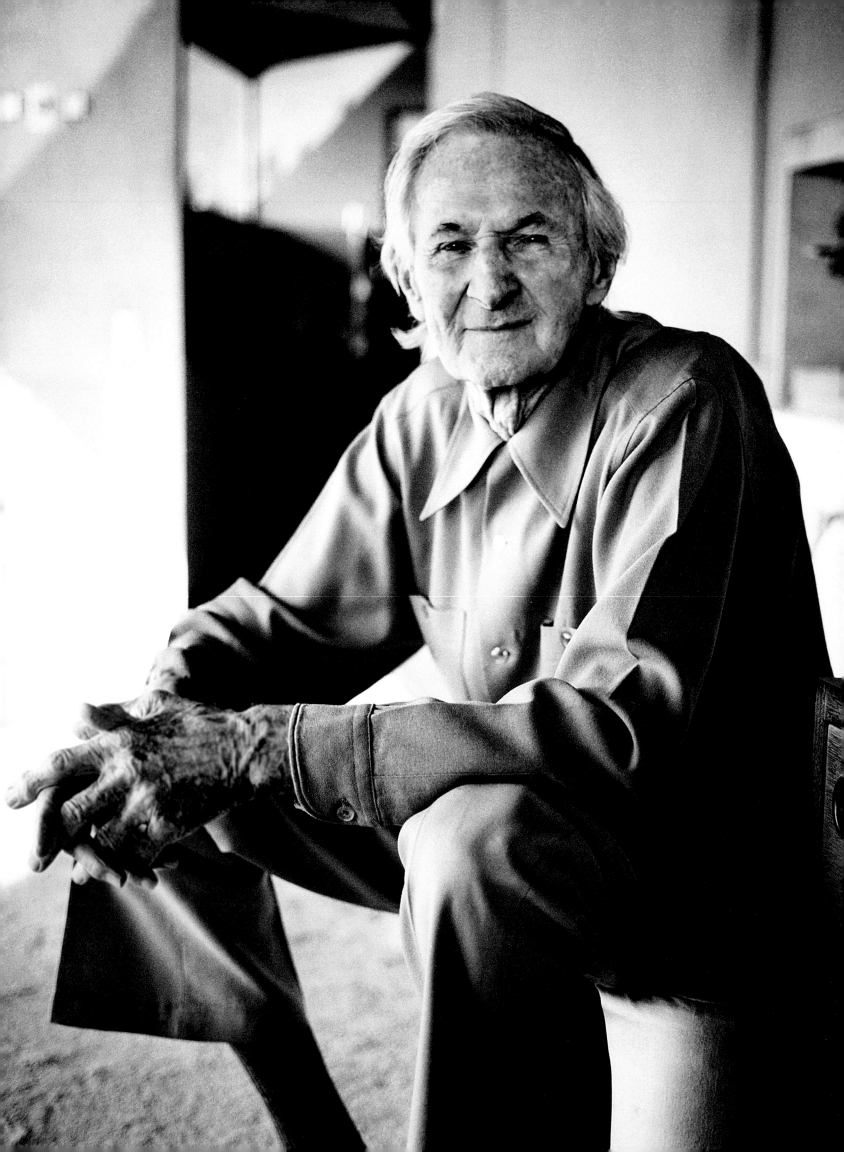

TEXTS

opposite:

FRANÇOIS HALARD

Portrait of Albert Frey, 1995

Courtesy of and © François Halard

FROM EAST TO WEST:
THE EXPERIMENTAL HOUSES OF ALBERT FREY

Joseph Rosa

Albert Frey would have been a significant figure in the history of American modern architecture even if he had never practiced on the West Coast. His East Coast work with A. Lawrence Kocher (from 1930 to 1934) produced two houses that are seminal examples of experimental American modern architecture—the 1931 Aluminaire House and the 1934 Kocher Canvas Week-End House (PP. 60–62). As Frey was also the first disciple of Le Corbusier to build in America, these houses reflected a Corbusian ideology of inventiveness, experimentation, and optimism that had never been seen before in the United States.[1] Frey was at Le Corbusier's atelier at a very formative time, from 1928 to 1929, and he worked on numerous noted projects; however, his most significant contribution was to the iconic 1929 Villa Savoye.[2] While at the atelier, Le Corbusier knew of Frey's intention to continue on to the United States and frequently referred to him as "this American guy."[3] Intermittently throughout the 1930s, Frey and Le Corbusier corresponded with each other, and Le Corbusier's words of support, "you see things . . . with personal vision, personal judgment and personal reactions," encouraged Frey to pursue modern architecture in America.[4]

Frey came to the United States in September 1930 and, shortly thereafter, started working with A. Lawrence Kocher.[5] Of their collaboration, it was commonly known that "Frey was the designer and Kocher was the writer and front man."[6] The 1931 Aluminaire House, one of the first projects to emerge from their partnership, is one of the earliest examples of modern architecture on the East Coast.[7] It was also one of the few buildings to represent the American modern movement at the acclaimed *International Exhibition of Modern Architecture*, curated by Henry-Russell Hitchcock and Philip Johnson, at the Museum of Modern Art in 1932. Of the six buildings from the United States subsequently included in the book *The International Style: Architecture Since 1922*, authored by Hitchcock and Johnson, only two were houses: Richard Neutra's 1929 Lovell House in Los Angeles and the 1931 Aluminaire House.[8]

opposite:

PRELIMINARY SKETCH

Aluminaire House (1930)

colored pencil on paper
ARCHITECTS: A. Lawrence Kocher with Albert Frey
Special Collections, John D. Rockefeller Jr. Library
The Colonial Williamsburg Foundation
A. Lawrence Kocher Collection, MS1986.12

The Aluminaire was first constructed as a full-scale model house—and was intended to be a prototype for mass-produced housing—for the *Allied Arts Exhibition* at the Grand Central Palace in New York in April 1931. The house's volume was predicated on the size of the atrium space in the exhibition hall.[9] It was erected in less than ten days and was the first house in America to be constructed solely from light steel and aluminum.[10] The first floor comprised an open-air porch, an entry, a dumbwaiter that serviced each level of the house, and a drive-through garage. The second floor was the only level that occupied the full envelope of the house. The living room was a two-story space with a seventeen-foot-high ceiling. The dining area was separated from the living room by a built-in glass and metal cabinet that housed an extendable dining table made of metal with a rubber top that retracted into a cylinder. The main bedroom, exercise room, and bathroom occupied a single space divided by a folding screen, and the beds were to be suspended from the ceiling. In the living room, multicolored neon-light tubes with reflectors were recessed into the ceiling above and in front of the two-story window. The third floor contained a library, a bathroom that projected into the two-story living room below, and a roof terrace. The walls, parapet, and partial roof plane of the roof terrace were sheathed in asbestos cement board, and the floor was covered in a resilient asphalt tile. The terrace was intended for various uses: a play area for children, a sleeping porch on summer nights, and an outdoor dining area.[11]

The Aluminaire's structure comprised six aluminum columns fastened to aluminum and light steel channel girders, which supported lightweight steel beams covered with battle-deck pressed steel flooring layered with insulation board and linoleum. None of the walls were load bearing; they acted as screens, and the interior wall surface was insulation board covered with "Fabrikoid"—a washable wall fabric that gave the appearance of a flat, jointless surface. All window sashes, doors, and frames were steel. The exterior wall assembly comprised narrow-ribbed aluminum with insulation board.[12] While some of these materials were not commercially available, they were intended to show what a "House for Contemporary Life" would be like, constructed from light metals and synthetic products that had proven their ability in other technical fields.[13]

At the close of the *Allied Arts Exhibition*, the architect Wallace K. Harrison purchased the house from Allied Arts. The Aluminaire was then dismantled and delivered to Harrison's estate on Long Island, where it was erected as a weekend home for his family. The photographs of the Aluminaire shown at the 1932 MoMA exhibition and frequently reprinted in books and magazines illustrating modern architecture in America show it standing on a knoll of the Harrison estate and not as it was first built, as a demonstration house to showcase new ideas and new American building materials.[14]

Shortly after the house was reassembled, Harrison built two one-story additions at either end of the garage, and the Aluminaire became the basis for Harrison's vast estate, with further additions. Eventually, in the early 1940s, the Aluminaire was moved from its original location at the top of a knoll to its base. The first floor was transformed into a basement, the entrance was moved to the second floor, and the third-floor exterior roof deck became a fully enclosed room with windows identical to the ones employed at the second floor. The Aluminaire, once poised elegantly at the top of its knoll, was now reduced to a "tin house," as Harrison referred to it, buried into the hillside and left to corrode for the next forty-five years.

While the Aluminaire House was a very important and iconic house, it seemed to have disappeared into the landscape of Long Island, New York. Scholars and historians knew of it, but no one knew its location or had actually seen it. When I was conducting research for my book *Albert Frey, Architect* (Rizzoli, 1990; German edition by Artemis, 1995; reprinted and designed by Princeton Architectural Press, 1999), it was essential to find it or better understand what happened to it. I was working in the architecture office of Peter D. Eisenman in New York in 1986, and one day, while talking with a colleague at the office, I expressed my frustration that this amazing house was somewhere on Long Island and nobody knew its location or its fate. After my colleague looked at the iconic 1932 photographs, she said to me, "I know the location of it—it's the tin house." She then explained to me that her father was an architect who had worked for Wallace Harrison and that she had grown up in a house on the same street as the main entrance to the vast Harrison estate. She drew me a map with its location on the Harrison property, and I rented a car the next day to go see it. When I arrived, I started walking up the driveway to the Harrison estate and saw the Aluminaire embedded into the side of the landscape. At that point, a neighbor from across the street asked me what I was doing, and I mentioned that my colleague—I said her name—told me of this house's location. The neighbor then said very nice things about my colleague's family and informed me that the new owner of the Harrison estate wanted to tear down the tin house and that the Huntington Historic Preservation Commission was having a public hearing the following week.

The Harrisons sold the estate in 1974 to their friend Hester Diamond, a highly regarded art collector and dealer. In 1984, Hester Diamond sold the Harrison estate to a doctor, and in 1986, the new owner requested a permit to demolish the house. At the time, the Aluminaire House was listed on the National Register of Historic Places as part of the Harrison estate, but to be protected, it required an individual listing with the Huntington Local Register of Historic Places. I attended the public hearings and spoke on the significance of the Aluminaire and the respective careers of Albert Frey and A. Lawrence Kocher. After that, I

179

reached out to the local newspaper to solicit support for saving the house and then reached out to the architects and scholars that supported my research on Frey and ask them to send letters. I also wrote a small news article about it for *Progressive Architecture* magazine (January 1987). Many letters of support came in to help save the structure from demolition. What was needed was an individual or an institution that would be willing to take it, dismantle it, and reconstruct it as it was originally intended.

Then a good friend said to me, "You need to bring this to Paul Goldberger's attention at the *New York Times*," and then introduced me to him. I met with him and shared my research on the Aluminaire House. Goldberger's essay in the Sunday *New York Times*, "Architecture View: Icon of Modernism Poised for Extinction" (March 7, 1987) was the gamechanger that saved the Aluminaire. Shortly thereafter, Jon Michael Schwarting, an architecture professor at New York Institute of Technology on Long Island, came forward and expressed interest in moving the house to the campus of its School of Architecture in Central Islip, where it would be used to teach students about the modern movement and early efforts in affordable housing. The owner then agreed to donate the house to NYIT and not demolish it. The school obtained a restoration grant from the New York State Department of Parks, Recreation, and Historic Preservation to cover the cost of relocation. By the fall of 1987, the Aluminaire House was officially saved from demolition and in the stewardship of NYIT under the direction of Schwarting and his colleague Frances Campani.[15]

Frey's experimentation with spatial configurations was further explored with the 1934 Kocher Canvas Weekend House, where the common living spaces—living, dining, and kitchen—are transformed into private spaces in the evenings. Constructed for Kocher as a weekend retreat for his family, the house was built in Northport, New York, about a mile from the shore, and it withstood a hurricane in 1938, only to be demolished by a developer in the late 1950s.[16] The house is similar in concept to Kocher and Frey's unbuilt 1932 Experiential Weekend House. The house comprised three levels, but only the second floor was enclosed, accessible by an exterior circulator stair that also serviced the roof deck. The ground floor provided shade and acted as the porch and garage, while the roof deck was used for sunbathing and outdoor sleeping. The second floor contained all the public and private spaces in one common area. A curtain track was mounted on the ceiling, and at night, the drapes from the perimeter windows were pulled into the center of the house, transforming the public living area into private sleeping spaces.

The Kocher Canvas Weekend House was supported by only six steel columns that carried wood-framed floors and walls. The exterior surfaces were composed of diagonal redwood sheathing that was coated with white lead to bond marine-treated canvas to the wood. The overlapping canvas pieces were applied horizontally, starting at the bottom of the wall, and nailed every six inches. It was then painted with three coats of oil-based paint before a finish coat was applied. The interior walls and ceiling were veneered plywood with a canvas floor. Aesthetically, the Kocher Canvas Weekend House was a totally non-representational object—the only thing that defined it as a house was its scale. The house also shows Frey's use of color that would be expanded upon in his later domestic projects. The envelope of the house was painted an aluminum color; the columns and railings were painted sage green; and the steel window frames, awning, and canvas interior floor were painted deep red.

In fall 1934, Frey left for Palm Springs to supervise the construction of the Kocher-Samson Building for A. Lawrence Kocher's brother. The building would be the last of their partnership. They had no new projects on the East Coast, and Frey had grown fond of the desert landscape and mountains of California, which reminded him of Switzerland. The dissolution of the studio was amicable.[17] Palm Springs had become the new frontier for Frey, and he could be a pioneer with a raw landscape. Frey met John Porter Clark when the Kocher-Samson Building was under construction. Clark and Frey established their studio shortly thereafter. Clark was educated at Cornell University and was the first architect to live and practice in Palm Springs.[18] From 1935 to 1937, Clark and Frey received numerous commissions, each designing their own projects. In many ways, Frey was trying to understand the desert landscape and how to design modern dwellings appropriate for this arid climate.

In 1937, Frey was contacted by Philip L. Goodwin, who was collaborating with Edward Durrell Stone on the Museum of Modern Art in New York City. Goodwin needed a designer who could produce designs within the idiom of the International Style.[19] Frey left the partnership with Clark and returned to New York. After the MoMA building was completed, Goodwin invited Frey to become a partner in the firm; however, Frey declined and, in 1939, returned to his partnership with Clark in Palm Springs that would last almost twenty years.[20] These two years away from Palm Springs were very formative time for Frey. He could see what his career and contribution to the field of architecture would be depending on if he stayed in New York or went back to Palm Springs. While Palm Springs was an arid desert, it had the potential to embrace a more experiential, inventive, and defining modern architecture—like Le Corbusier's vision for Chandigarh—than a well-established city like New York did. Frey saw what was happening in Los Angeles and knew that ambition and growth could happen in the desert. Frey also had the time to formulate what an architecture for the desert might be, and the projects he designed for this arid climate would have the same strength as his earlier East Coast work.

The one element that unites Frey's earlier East Coast and later West Coast works is his inventiveness with new materials and experimentation with new spatial relationships. Frey's desert architecture—from the 1940s on—addressed the issues of sun, temperature, and prevailing winds. Using materials that work best in the desert from a functional and aesthetic point of view, he created a modern architecture that was firmly rooted in Le Corbusier's rhetoric and adapted it to this environment. His East Coast work is radically different in composition from his West Coast, evolving from pure, non-representational volumes raised off the ground plane to simple rectilinear compositions of horizontal wall planes that extend out into the desert landscape. Frey's best example of this thinking can be seen in the 1940 design for his own house.

The plan for Frey House I (PP. 88–105) was a rectangle only sixteen by twenty feet, comprising a kitchen, bathroom, and a multipurpose living room/bedroom that opened to the pool beyond. It was standard wood-frame construction cladded with four-by-eight-foot panels, and the walls of the house were a series of planes that engaged a large square roof surface that enforced the horizontal movement of these walls into the landscape and acted as overhang to create shade. The walls that extended beyond the envelope of the house and into the landscape act as screens to separate different outdoor activities, just like interior walls do. The envelope of Frey House I was sheathed with corrugated metal, which was applied vertically to the static perimeter walls and horizontally on the wall surfaces that extended into the landscape. All interior wall surfaces were colored asbestos cement board fastened with exposed screws. In keeping with the compact nature of the design, Frey incorporated light fixtures into the walls and covered them with ventilation grills to direct the lighting. This minimalist strategy can also be seen in the seating around the pool embedded into the concrete, thereby fixing the views framed by each seat. The color palette of Frey House I reflected his interest in the flora and fauna of the desert environment. The exterior wall material was corrugated metal and left unpainted. The corrugated metal ceiling plane was painted a light blue, and the asbestos cement board walls were either pale green or rose. All the window frames were pale yellow, and the fascia trim—at the edge of the ceiling plane—was painted white.

More traditionally styled houses in the desert were built of wood-framed construction clad with wire lath and stucco for their walls. The sheathing of a wood-framed structure with corrugated metal challenged the normative building vocabulary in the desert while furthering the notion of a house being, as Le Corbusier would say, a "Machine for Living" in the rugged arid terrain. Frey House I was an important contribution, placing Palm Springs's domestic architecture on the map as a new frontier for the modern idiom and appearing in magazines such as *Architectural Forum, Architectural Record, Domus, House and Garden,* and *Werk* and in books such as *The Modern House in America* by Katherine and James Ford and *A Decade of New Architecture* edited by Sigfried Giedon.

The notoriety Frey House I received, however, did not deter Frey from using his house as a laboratory to further explore new ideas and materials on the market.[21] In 1948, Frey added a more defined living room with an interior/ exterior pool. His later additions and alterations in 1953 transformed the house from a one-story Miesian/De Stijl composition into an expressionist assemblage of inventive explorations. In architectural historian David Gebhard's book, *A Guide to Architecture in Southern California*, he endearingly referred to the home as "Frey's Flash Gordon" house and for good reason.[22] A bedroom was added to the second floor that was round in plan and had round windows. This new exterior form was sheathed in diamond-patterned aluminum. To provide sunscreens for these windows, Frey designed round awnings for all of them. The round second-floor addition with round windows gave more of an impression of a telescope or observation deck than it did a private retreat. The interior of this expansion was equally over the top. The interior walls were covered in yellow tufted vinyl fabric, and the drapes were electric blue vinyl. Stairs up to the bedroom and a round dining room table suspended from the ceiling by aluminum rods added to the futuristic atmosphere. As other houses were going up around House I, Frey enclosed the outdoor pool area with a curvilinear wall made of corrugated fiberglass and metal.

In the later years of his career, Frey returned to simpler forms of structure and enclosure that further integrated the houses into the landscape. Although these later houses are mostly pure structure wrapped in glass, Frey used the unique characteristics of each site to create spatial conditions that were contextual in a way his earlier East Coast work was not. His second home for himself—Frey House II (PP. 144–161)—is the only built example of his adaptation of the modern idiom to the mountain terrain.

The 1964 Frey House II sites on a steep hill—220 feet above Palm Springs— with natural rock outcroppings. While the house itself is a very simple minimalist composition, its relationship to the site, as well as the grid of the city below, is complex. A platform, which is parallel to the road, projects beyond the house and acts as a deck for the pool and as a roof for the carport below. The house is situated three steps higher than the deck and is on an east-west axis in relationship to the rectilinear, man-made grid imposed on the desert below. The platform is placed in relationship to the natural contours of the mountain, and the teardrop shape of the pool is the result of the interaction of these two different orders.

The platform is constructed of colored poured concrete and concrete block to allow it to blend in with the mountain; the house, which stands in contrast to it, is a simple rectangle with one common space comprising the living, dining, and sleeping areas. Although the house seems, at first, to have no relationship to the site, it is firmly rooted in the mountain and interacts literally with the landscape. This can be seen as the elevation of the floor changes with the natural grade at the dining area, and a large boulder penetrating the glass wall visually anchors the house to the site. The ceiling plane is also angled to accommodate the boulder, which acts as a focal point in the plan of the house with each of the built-in-cabinet units radiating out from it and defining the dining, living, and sleeping areas. The house is steel-frame construction with spans of glass and colored corrugated aluminum exterior walls. The interior walls are smooth finished-grade plywood veneer, and the roof is an enameled ribbed metal that blends in with the color of the rocks. Over the decades, the house has weathered the arid climate beautifully and has needed minimal maintenance. Frey saw the desert as a tabula rasa and created a modern architecture that embraced life in the desert and the materials needed to achieve that vision.

One can trace the evolution in Frey's thinking from the 1931 Aluminaire House, conceived devoid of an actual site, to his refined 1964 Frey House II that is highly contextual to its site. What ties together the design of the four houses discussed here is Frey's ongoing experimentation with materials and the reductive nature of these interiors. Frey is one of the few architects that had two vastly different highly acclaimed practices that happened on two different coasts, in different decades, and with different scales of work. However, Frey's East Coast work was essential in the development of his ideology and architectural vocabulary that later laid the groundwork for his West Coast work. Born in Switzerland, a disciple of Le Corbusier, and designer of modern architecture on the East Coast, Frey brought a unique perspective to all his designs for the desert region of California and was a key figure in establishing the architectural idiom of desert modernism, as evidenced by a renewed interest in Frey's work and in Palm Springs as a mecca for mid-century modern architecture.

NOTES

1. Hamilton Beatty and Norman N. Rice, both Americans, worked for Le Corbusier and Pierre Jeanneret, his cousin and atelier partner. Rice started in the fall of 1929, Beatty in the fall of 1930, and both were back in the United States by 1931. Rice worked in the studio of Howe & Lescaze on the PSFS and wrote articles for *Architectural Forum* and *Shelter* magazines. Rice did not build his own work until the late 1930s. Beatty built his first structure, a house, in the late summer of 1931 in Madison, Wisconsin, in collaboration with his wife Gwendydd. Joseph Rosa interview with Bill Strauss (nephew and holder of Norman N. Rice papers), May 16, 1989; Joseph Rosa interview with Hamilton Beatty, May 22, 1989; Le Corbusier black logbook, Fondation Le Corbusier.

2. Joseph Rosa, interviews with Albert Frey, July 18 and 19, 1987; Fondation Le Corbusier, Le Corbusier atelier black logbook. The black logbook was used in the atelier to record most of the drawings that were done and usually was signed by the draftsman that drew the drawings. Frey prepared almost all the construction drawings for Villa Savoye. Back logbook nos. 2036, 2039, 2089, 2122, 2131, 2136, 2137, 2138, 2141, 2146, 2148, 2152, 2160, 2162, 2171, and 2172.

3. Joseph Rosa interview with Albert Frey, July 27, 1987.

4. Letter from Le Corbusier to Albert Frey, October 26, 1934. Fondation Le Corbusier. Translation by Sandra-Lisa Forman.

5. Since their office consisted solely of Frey and Kocher, Frey worked on the projects at the office during the day while Kocher was at *Architectural Record*. In the evenings, they would discuss the progress of the work. Joseph Rosa, interview with Albert Frey, November 16, 1986.

6. Joseph Rosa interview with Philip Johnson, May 28, 1987.

7. Tim Benton, *The Villas of Le Corbusier 1920–1930* (New Haven: Yale University Press, 1987), 205.

8. Richard Guy Wilson, Dianne H. Pilgrim, and Dickran Tashjian, *The Machine Age* (New York: Brooklyn Museum and Abrams, 1986), 170. For more on the history of the exhibition, see Terence Riley's book *International Style: Exhibition 15 and The Museum of Modern Art* (New York: Rizzoli and Columbia Books of Architecture, 1992).

9. Joseph Rosa, interview with Albert Frey, November 14, 1986.

10. A. Lawrence Kocher Papers, and F. R. S. Yorke, *The Modern House* (London: The Architectural Press, 1934), 181–82.

11. Joseph Rosa, interview with Albert Frey, July 25,1987.

12. Yorke, *The Modern House*, 181.

13. "Aluminaire: A House for Contemporary Life," *Shelter* (May 1932), 58.

14. Victoria Newhouse, *Wallace K. Harrison, Architect* (New York: Rizzoli, 1989), 60; Mrs. Wallace K. Harrison, letter to Joseph Rosa, May 20, 1987.

15. Joseph Rosa interview with Hester Diamond, June 6, 1987; interview with Michael Lynch, restoration coordinator of grants for the New York State Department of Parks, Recreation and Historic Preservation, May 26, 1989; interview with Jon Michael Schwarting, New York Institute of Technology, School of Architecture, June 8, 1989.

16. Joseph Rosa, interview with Marge Kocher, September 15, 1987.

17. Joseph Rosa, interview with Albert Frey, November 16, 1987.

18. Joseph Rosa, interview with John Porter Clark, October 18, 1987.

19. Frey was recommended to Goodwin by Alfred Clauss. Clauss was the first disciple of Mies van der Rohe to come to America. Clauss and Frey met at William Lescaze's office in New York and became best friends. From July 1931 to July 1932, the projects in the Kocher and Frey studio were sparse, and to make ends meet, Frey worked part time as a designer for William Lescaze. Frey designed Lescaze's earlier proposal for the Museum of Modern Art (scheme 5 & 6, 1931). Frey later introduced Clauss to Jane West. She was the first American woman to work for Le Corbusier. She returned to the United States in 1932. Alfred and Jane married in 1934. Joseph Rosa, interview with Alfred and Jane West Clauss, May 19, 1987; Joseph Rosa, interview with Albert Frey, August 15, 1987.

20. In 1952, Robson Chambers was made a partner and the firm name was changed to Clark, Frey, and Chambers. Then, in 1956, Clark left the firm to establish his own solo practice, and the name was changed again to Frey and Chambers. In 1966, Chambers left the office and relocated to Santa Barbara, California, and Frey reduced the scope of the office to be mostly residential projects. Joseph Rosa, interview with Robson Chambers, November 7, 1987; Joseph Rosa, interview with Frey, August 15, 1987; Joseph Rosa, interview with Clark, October 18, 1987.

21. Joseph Rosa interview with Albert Frey, November 1, 1987.

22. David Gebhard, *A Guide to Architecture in Southern California* (Los Angeles: Los Angeles County Museum of Art, 1965).

23. Joseph Rosa, email to authors, May 17, 2023.

opposite:

MAGAZINE FEATURE

Aluminaire House (1930)

Popular Mechanics, August 1931
ARCHITECTS: A. Lawrence Kocher with Albert Frey
Courtesy of Palm Springs Art Museum, Hyman Library

the FUTURE

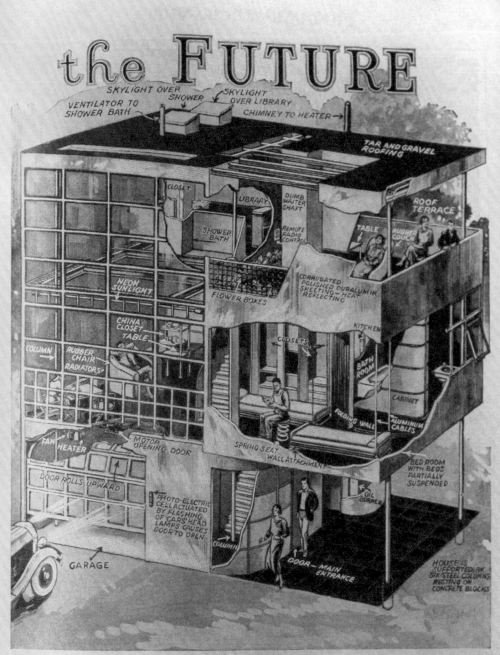

SKYLIGHT OVER SHOWER — SKYLIGHT OVER LIBRARY
VENTILATOR TO SHOWER BATH — CHIMNEY TO HEATER →
TAR AND GRAVEL ROOFING
CLOSET
LIBRARY
DUMB WAITER SHAFT
ROOF TERRACE
SHOWER BATH
REMOTE RADIO CONTROL
TABLE
RUBBER COUCH
NEON SUNLIGHT
FLOWER BOXES
CORRUGATED POLISHED DURALUMIN SHEETING — HEAT REFLECTING
CHINA CLOSET TABLE
KITCHEN
CLOSETS
COLUMN →
RUBBER CHAIR RADIATORS
BATH ROOM
CABINET
FOLDING WALL
ALUMINUM CABLES
FAN HEATER
MOTOR OPENING DOOR
SPRING SEAT WALL ATTACHMENT
BED ROOM WITH BEDS PARTIALLY SUSPENDED
DOOR ROLLS UPWARD
PHOTO-ELECTRIC CELL ACTUATED BY FLASHING OF CARS HEAD LAMPS CAUSES DOOR TO OPEN
OIL BURNER
COLUMN
GARAGE
DOOR — MAIN ENTRANCE
HOUSE IS SUPPORTED BY SIX STEEL COLUMNS RESTING ON CONCRETE BLOCKS

Drawn by Logan U. Reaves

Cut-Away Representation of the Home of the Future; the House Is Constructed Entirely of Metal and Glass, with the Latest Space and Labor-Saving Features

ing room, the foundry, laboratory and the brain of man.

As it stood at the exposition, this house represented the effort of centuries, although it cost only $4,000.

The ground dimensions are twenty-two by twenty-eight feet and the height is thirty-five feet. The house has no basement, because, according to the architect, basements are hold-overs from the days before mechanical refrigeration, when foods were kept cool underground.

As for convenience and comfort, this house embodies almost everything man has so far devised to add to his ease. It might be regarded as a sort of museum of domestic invention. The architect conceived it on the principle that moderns want luxury at moderate prices, not merely quaint, vine-clad cottages.

DESERT ENCOUNTERS:
FREY, NEUTRA, AND SCHINDLER IN *DIE WÜSTE*

Barbara Lamprecht

Albert Frey (1903–1998) is so widely beloved that it would be hubris to present something portending to be original. This, then, is a more personal recasting of what we know of Frey's own response to the desert, profoundly different than those of his fellow European Modernists, Rudolf Schindler (1887–1953) or Richard Neutra (1892–1970), who also designed seminal projects in the Coachella Valley.

Frey was not an idealogue. Rather, he radiated a refreshing attitude about architecture and life. Luxury had nothing to do with wealth. Simplicity liberated, as his own life personified. Recounted many times and not here, his extraordinary repertoire demonstrates his genius and agility in resolving design questions a priori, as well as an unwavering commitment to the promise of industrial materials to deliver humane design economically.

There is something ineffably happy about Frey's work, reflecting a curiosity unfettered by polemics. This is a man who told me he tested the deflection of the joists for his first house by hanging from them, but that is not to suggest he experimented ad-hoc. Frey's early training reveals much about him and his love of materials: as a teenager, he built canoes of wood and canvas. He appropriated his mother's old gloves to build bellows for a camera he invented.[1] His university curriculum in Zurich was oriented to technics, not design, but as Frey scholar Joseph Rosa has noted, Frey quickly immersed himself in new thinking: the Bauhaus, Mies Van der Rohe, DeStijl, and his great mentor Le Corbusier.

Frey arrived in Palm Springs in late October 1934 to oversee the construction of the Kocher-Samson Building, having visited Los Angeles in 1932 to see the work of Neutra, Schindler, and others. Both Schindler and Neutra had completed their masterpieces, the Lovell Beach House (1926) and the Lovell Health House (1929), respectively. They had already worked in the desert,

opposite:

STEPHEN H. WILLARD

Kocher-Samson Building (1934)

ARCHITECTS: A. Lawrence Kocher and Albert Frey
Palm Springs Art Museum
Albert Frey Collection, 55-1999.2, VIIB45-5

189

and their projects not only exploded encrusted desert architectural mores but also reinforced the personas and work of these two men, friends from their early days in Vienna, as absolute opposites: Modernism's id and super-ego, its Apollo and Dionysus.

Schindler's mostly unrealized desert projects were often commissioned by individuals who were free, bold, and paper-thin in resources. They sought isolated sites in the Coachella Valley, well away from public view. He designed a tiny cabin in Indio for Paul and Betty Popenoe (now demolished) with an "absolutely essential" budget of $2,000 in 1922, the same year he completed his own home, the Kings Road House in Los Angeles.[3]

Against that experimental concrete, glass, and redwood house, the Indio cabin—a squarish wooden box surrounded by a rambling array of screened outdoor rooms—was frail by comparison. The central room projects above the rest of the house, recalling the influence of Schindler's early mentor, the notorious Adolf Loos (1870–1933), whose concept of *Raumplan* reflected the hierarchy of social space: more important public/communal rooms commanded taller ceilings.[4] One detail, easy to overlook at first, shocks and then educates. The western side of one outdoor room is sheathed in vertically oriented palm fronds. They must have rustled and murmured while acting as a privacy screen and wind break, just as a "skirt" of palm fronds functions in indigenous California fan palms, *Washingtonia filifera*, found in oases throughout Coachella Valley. This detail speaks eloquently to Schindler's full-throated embrace of the desert, seeking out its native technologies and adapting them for human use.

Completed twenty-five years later, the Maryon Toole House (1947) in Palm Desert (formerly Palm Village) is the only remaining Schindler project in the Coachella Valley, and it is spectacular. The Toole House recalls Frank Lloyd Wright's plays on 30/60 angles and his earthy strategies but is very much Schindler's own version of "breaking the box": in a way, it's more lizard than house in its sticky grasp of the ground. Angles converge and diverge. Low to the ground, a series of three overlapping, boomerang-shaped wood roofs shelter walls of burnished desert rocks embedded in concrete; this "spotted wall" recalls a cheetah's skin, simultaneously visually standing out and disappearing into the landscape.[5] To the east, the roofs slide out from one another and stretch out into the desert, ending in full-height walls of glass opening out to an outdoor terrace. The low-pitched wood roofs, whose gables are also glass, seem to float above the solid walls, which slightly extend beyond the roofline. "The whole is shaded by an ample but lightly poised roof reminiscent of a giant leaf," Schindler said of his foliated roof design.[6] Now being restored, the house exemplifies Schindler's sense of romance and emotion in his feeling for the desert.

If Schindler's thinking seemed to embody a sacred native spirt, absolutely in tune with the desert's profundities, Neutra proudly acknowledged his architecture as Other. In *Wie Baut Amerika* (How America Builds), his 1927 book published in Germany, endless pictures of steel skyscraper framing and details boast an America bristling with the future of new technologies. At the book's end, however, the tenor changes abruptly. Now a few pictures of adobe pueblo dwellings percolate the remaining text, yet another strange American phenomenon, Neutra might have thought, sure to impress a naïve European audience.[7] And as though an afterthought, he included plans and photos of Schindler's twelve-unit Pueblo Ribera, La Jolla (1923), a project of redwood, sand, and concrete made from beach sand. Likewise, Lloyd Wright's Oasis Hotel, Palm Springs (1924), earned a photo, as did Wright's concrete "knit-block" Storer House, Los Angeles (1923)—all three a world away from Neutra's obvious admiration for Chicago skyscrapers. The very last image in *Wie Baut Amerika* is the climax concluding this sudden change in emphasis: no buildings, no big pieces of float glass, no steel, just ribbons of sand melting into the horizon. The caption reads, "Die primitive Wüstenlandschaft."

That last word is often translated as "desert," but the word is much deeper etymologically. It conveys barrenness, wasteland, a place so wild as to be inhumane.[8] His use of the phrase is telling: for all the deserved fame of the Kaufmann Desert House (1946) as one of the twentieth century's seminal houses, the house embodies his own, and very un-Wrightian, definition of "organic." "Any pretense that buildings are rooted or draw nourishment from the ground or moisture from the soil. . . is poetic metaphor at best and misleading at worst," he wrote.[9] The Desert House, he wrote, was "inserted" into this harsh backdrop, "set on footings," whose juxtaposition of artifice and artificial climate underscored "the weather, the silver-white moonlight, and the starry sky." To Neutra, "organic" meant understanding that a human's biology and psychology and humanity's common evolutionary history were paramount to designing for well-being. For Neutra, that was architecture's raison d'etre, not self-expression.

The Popenoes and Ms. Toole couldn't have been more different than Edgar J. Kaufmann, the department store magnate who demanded nothing less than a world-class house for his winter sojourns.[10] The metal louvers employed throughout the house were his agile response to the same harsh desert winds that prompted Schindler's wall of palm fronds.[11] And by contrast to the Lovell Health House, where the glass windows of Philip and Leah Lovell's master bedroom face south and west with a shallow overhang on the south (meaning a possibly brutal afternoon and evening of solar gain), Edgar and Lillian's bedroom face due east and morning light, sheltered by a broad overhang.

Completed in 1937, Neutra's other desert project, the Grace Lewis Miller House, is much closer to the native architecture of the Southwest than the Kaufmann villa. While the Miller's white volumes and simple materials readily recall pueblo dwellings, it was Neutra's synthesis of that native building type, the severity of the International Style, and his deployment of a full repertoire of his signature strategies, including a reflecting pool with its dances of light and shadow, that has ensured its permanent acclaim.

Neutra populated both of his Palm Springs settings with careful transitions between house and *die Wüste*. At the Miller House, a border of jagged, flat Salton Sea stones defined the boundary between the irrigated patch of grass lawn (sown with seeds "imported" from St. Louis) and the untamed desert beyond.[12] The border is the liminal space between *die Wüste* and suburban domesticity, acknowledging that tension. At the Kaufmann Desert House, the landscape, too, is humanmade: perfectly sized and placed boulders cascade down a sloping carpet of green lawn interspersed with palm trees—all artifice.

We know that all design is artifice to one degree or another. Neutra emphasized that his architecture was "foreign," a foil to the surroundings that enriched a dialectic between the two. Schindler did not acknowledge the relevance of such a dialectic, rather, a profound rapport. As for Albert Frey, he had other questions, other concerns, other agendas.

The Kocher-Samson building and the Guthrie House that soon followed in 1935 were very much International Style, meaning boxy white volumes that were stacked and offset to create shade, rather than using a very different strategy for shade of thin overhangs that extended a roofline.[13] In later projects, this changed, when Frey and architect John Porter Clark, his partner from 1939 to 1957, began working together. For example, they mounted a ten-foot pole at the center of a circle, like a sundial, to resolve the depth of overhangs at different sun exposures. For Frey House II (1963) (PP. 144–161), his 800-square-foot glass and steel jewel box cradled into a pink concrete block frame high on the slopes of Mount San Jacinto, Frey worked on the problem for a year.[14] He sited his second home north-south to provide for passive solar gain in the winter; in summer, cross ventilation tempers the relentless heat.

Frey House II's massive menhir straddling indoors and out seems to hover momentarily, as if suspended in time. Dramatic, of course, but this rock has real work to do. Its huge mass radiates warmth on winter nights; spatially, the rock distinguishes bedroom from living space. In the harsh, seesaw climate of Palm Springs, Frey's distrust of wood, plaster, and composite roofs in favor of the lean resilience of metal, of steel columns and powder-coated aluminum siding and concrete, were logical materials to him. The terrace, a tear-shaped pool, follows the contours of the land. The house steps up, just as the hill does. Demonstrating the material's plasticity, concrete projections in the steps form sensuous outdoor seating, recalling Le Corbusier's famous built-in chaise longue in the Villa Savoye's bathroom, which Frey may well have worked on. Notably, where Corbu's chaise longue is tiled, leaving the viewer to wonder what, exactly, is supporting it and whether anyone ever actually splayed out on this throne to Eros, Frey's friendly, sunny seating tames concrete and rankly expresses the material and its function. Stepping up into the house, a similar concrete projection supports the plywood seating, the back of which, in turn, functions as bookcase and dining table, one end free to take his left-handed T-square. "I liked that idea," he said, running his hands along its edge. "You don't have to put [in] a framework to put it on. It's much cleaner that way." [15]

I first met Frey in 1990, in Frey House II, his solitary sanctuary far removed from the city below. He aligned his home with the city's grid and with the city hall he designed in 1952, a choice that speaks to an architect's love of playing off datum lines. My first question was, "Why here?" The tall man with the pale yellow short-sleeved shirt looked down at me with a courtly, patient expression. "Why, because architecture is about light and shadow, and the desert is all about light and shadow," he exclaimed, as though surprised that an architecture student should ask such a question. "Switzerland was boring," he added encouragingly. I asked him about the blue corrugated ceiling: "Why, it's because of the Renaissance. You see all these blue ceilings, their white clouds, the angels. . . . I did not want the bright aluminum, which could be disturbing." [16]

I was taken aback. In two sentences, he shattered my naivete about what a stern canonical Modernist should be or should love.

He pickled the Philippine mahogany woodwork white with a Cabot stain (the same Boston manufacturer that brothers Charles and Henry Greene used for their Craftsman masterpieces decades earlier) because of his concern for the eye's physical comfort. "The iris should not be shocked when it moves from the bright desert sun to the interior of the house"—a statement Neutra could have made. [17] Frey loved yellow and blue, I learned, and many other colors as well, such as a sage green—all colors of the desert flowers. The copper brown of the slanted Cor-ten roof exactly matches the dark "desert burn" of the rocks lying on the mountainside. Even Frey's wardrobe "demonstrated a sensual notion of esthetic frugality. He wore shirts, trousers, and socks in a strictly limited palette of white, powder blue, salmon, pale yellow, and beige." [18]

While Frey may be best known for his singular buildings, from the beginning, housing was a continuing interest. The Aluminaire House (1930) (PP. 42–51), designed with A. Lawrence Kocher, is renowned as the country's first all-metal house (Neutra's Lovell Health House (1929) was the first steel-*framed* residence.) Today, the Aluminaire is one of Modernism's milestones, but it was always intended to be part of a low-cost housing project, much in the spirit of the early movement's earnest social ideals. As published in *The Architectural Record*, April 1931, the tract's layout shows that house as one of many identical homes, here staggered and rotated, providing privacy amidst gardens and trees that populated the tract. Frey realized this idea in his fifteen-unit Bel Vista tract (1946) in northern Palm Springs, and if most of what one knows of Frey is the astonishing Frey House II, it's hard to recognize these as his work. No dazzling steel, aluminum, or canvas, no Corbusian piloti, no Renaissance blue corrugated ceilings.

Bel Vista was constructed to be affordable for World War II workers. The flat-roofed, 1,120-square-foot modest structures sit firmly on the ground, built with standard wood framing and stucco. Overhangs shelter shallow, recessed, and projecting sections of these essentially square houses—in this regard, resembling Schindler's square Popenoe Cabin with its wandering overhangs and porches. Bel Vista's interiors speak to Frey's sense of economy: a hallway wrapping the central mechanical and storage core allows ready access to any part of the house. In this small house, seven doors provide access to the outdoors, an extraordinary luxury for "basic" dwellings. It's a choice that speaks to Frey's belief that everyone needed to be connected to nature and that each person should be able to determine their own path of travel. Outside, in one home, sections of the original sage green corrugated fencing remain. This familiar Frey trademark is perhaps the only obvious link to him unless one knows about another signature strategy, his love of contrast in shapes: one door leads to the outdoor laundry line, hidden from view by a semicircular wall of basket-weave brick, a curve made more vibrant amidst the right angles.[19]

Frey designed that theory of contrasts into the hardscape and second story of Frey House I (PP. 88–105), which started out as a 320-square-foot house in 1941, enlarged in 1947 and 1957. The swimming pool was lassoed by a sweeping, curvilinear screen wall of corrugated metal and fiberglass sheathing in overlapping panels of red and yellow, resulting in a patchwork quilt of colors.

But curves had other functions apart from aesthetically animating a project. As he explained,

> *Because of the contour of the curve, the wall is self-supporting. That was a wonderful thing. I have a few struts, three-quarter inch pipes, but that's all. So I get a wall that's less than a sixteenth of an inch thick and it supports itself! That's what I'm after, you see, to preserve material, to use the least possible amount. There should always be economy in cost. . . . Economy is always important because if people can't afford it, it's not a solution.* [20]

Frey celebrated such contrasts in his primer, *In Search of a Living Architecture*. After he briefly introduces five concerns—The Evolution of Architectural Form, Shape, Space, Composition, and Form in Nature—what follows illuminates those concerns. Each two-page spread thereafter is a short lesson in architecture. On the left is a photograph, anything from a natural feature to a group of water tanks, to Mont St. Michel, to a pueblo, to even a dirigible and a cantilevered diving board. Each right-hand page shows a response to those patterns, rhythms, materials, and forms that acquits a human need in new ways with new materials. These responses range from Giuseppe Terragni's brilliant Casa del Fascio, Como, Italy (1936) to Neutra's VDL Research House, Los Angeles (1932). What captured my attention, however, is a third, quite small figure on the spread: Frey's distillation of the parti into a simple diagram that bridges the ideas behind the two images. He discusses the psychological and emotional implications of those forms and contrasts of open and closed, curved and straight, tall and short, old and new. The book invites, never coerces, an understanding of the promise of Modernism, just as Frey's architecture does.

While this essay doesn't trace the nature of such influences or claim that linear relationships exist at all, a few observations do come to mind.

One might expect that Schindler would have visited Taliesin West (Taliesin III), Scottsdale (1937) with its low rock-and-cement walls, angles, and its intense response to the desert landscape, qualities not dissimilar to Schindler's intimate response to the desert seen in the Toole House. Architect, engineer, and inventor Walter S. White (1917–2002) worked for Schindler for eighteen months (1937–38) and for Clark and Frey between 1947 and '48, both offices where curiosity and experimentation were the default setting. White's roofs, hyperparabolic (spectacularly exuberant at the Willcockson House, Indio [1959]) or voluptuously curved (as seen at the now restored Miles Bates House [1953]), precede Frey's Tramway Station (1964). Frey's center pivoting windows for Frey House I (1935) might have inspired White's own center-pivoting "Solar Heat Exchanger Window Wall," patented in 1975. William Krisel (1924–2017), another of the city's famous sons, acknowledged Le Corbusier's 1930 unbuilt scheme for a Chilean heiress as Krisel's inspiration for his own butterfly roof, the shape that Krisel made famous in his fab tract we know and love today as Twin Palms. For El Pueblo Ribera, his beachfront development, Schindler took one standard unit and rotated and flipped it so that each unit enjoys a unique, and private, relationship to views and to gardens, just as Frey did at Bel Vista in 1946 and Krisel did at Twin Palms a decade later. Arriving to visit Neutra after graduating from the University of Minnesota and landing a job that afternoon, Don Wexler, Palm Spring's king of residential steel, worked for Neutra in 1951 before departing for Palm Springs in 1952. He would have known about, and doubtless visited and admired, the Lovell Health House. Neutra, in turn, worked on those Chicago skyscrapers, an experience that girded him with the courage to build the outrageous Lovell Health House that is barely tethered to a hill.

And so it goes. Frey, like Schindler and Neutra before him, encountered the desert. They brought their ideas, their imagination, and their values to the uncompromising *Wüste*, and each responded to the environment—drawing on the history of Modernist architecture in the desert and elsewhere that preceded them—on his own terms. We celebrate each on his own terms as well.

NOTES

1. Joseph Rosa, *Albert Frey, Architect* (New York: Rizzoli, 1990), 12–15.

2. The author wishes to acknowledge and thank scholar Luke Leuschner, who was exceptionally generous in sharing his research. His forthcoming book will thoroughly explore Schindler's work in the Coachella Valley.

3. Paul Popenoe (1888–1979) was initially a respected agricultural expert who cultivated exotic date species and added to the family's business founded by his father, Frederick Popenoe, a pioneer of the avocado industry. Paul Popenoe became known in later decades as a eugenicist intent on the segregation of "waste humanity." Still later, he became nationally famous as a marriage counselor, establishing the iconic "Can This Marriage Be Saved?" column in the *Ladies Home Journal*, launched in 1953 and continuing well into the 2000s. The "absolutely essential" limit of $2,000 is part of a May 5, 1922, letter from Popenoe to Schindler, R. M. Schindler Papers.

4. In effect, *Raumplan* resembled Frank Lloyd Wright's use of compression and expansion, i.e., entering a space with a low or dark ceiling and walking into a taller, light-filled space.

5. Michael Darling, "The Vulnerable Architecture of R. M. Schindler," in *The Architecture of R. M. Schindler*, ed. by Elizabeth A. T. Smith and Michael Darling (Los Angeles: Museum of Contemporary Art with Harry N. Abrams, 2001), 204.

6. Ibid.

7. These are possibly some of the haunting 400-odd snapshots that Rudolf Schindler took on his 1915 road trip through the Southwest. That summer, he tramped through the Grand Canyon and visited Taos, New Mexico, on a rail ticket. His photos captured low, asymmetric pueblo masses rising from the desert floor; the intense chiaroscuro of light and dark on a late afternoon; and Native women and men in tribal dress.

8. Neutra also dramatically called the Coachella Valley the "Badlands of the Cordillera." Badlands is a term for inhospitable and rough geography torn up by pinnacles and gullies.

9. Barbara Lamprecht, *Richard Neutra – Complete Works* (Koln, Los Angeles: Taschen, 2000), 52. Quote is from unpublished, undated manuscript, "Architecture and the Landscape," UCLA Special Collections, Charles E. Young Library, Richard Joseph Neutra Papers, Manuscript Collection 1179.

10. Kaufmann, of course, was accustomed to the best, hiring Frank Lloyd Wright for Falling Water, Bears Run, Pennsylvania (1935).

11. In his 2021 essay "Neutra and Brazil," Raymond Neutra, Richard and Dione's youngest son, writes that Neutra "visited the Los Eucaliptus apartment house designed by Jorge Ferrari Hardoy and Kurchan in 1941, where he was introduced to the idea of vertical rotating louvers that in turn were designed by another architect Villalobos."

12. Stephen Leet, *Richard Neutra's Miller House* (New York: Princeton Architectural Press, 2004), 126. See also Barbara Lamprecht, "The Landscaping Cannot Come Later: Richard Neutra's Faith in Landscape," *Eden* 23, no. 4 (Fall 2020) 4–29.

13. Although appearing to be a standard wood-frame-and-stucco building, the Kocher-Samson's construction is a progressive hybrid of concrete, metal decking, and lightweight steel frames, complete with a very unapologetic X- brace of two steel tie rods in the picture window facing the street.

14. Email correspondence with Sidney Williams, former curator of Architecture and Design, Palm Springs Art Museum, March 4, 2023. Williams noted Jennifer Golub's *Albert Frey Houses 1+2* (Princeton: Princeton Architectural Press, 1998), which includes the image of Frey's sun device.

15. Barbara Lamprecht interview with Albert Frey, Oct. 3, 1991.

16. Neil Jackson and Barbara Lamprecht, "Desert Pioneer," *The Architectural Review* (Sep. 1992) 40–44.

17. Ibid.

18. The author thanks historian and realtor Todd Hays for access to his two Bel Vista homes. Hays authored a nomination to the first Bel Vista home he meticulously restored, and he is now rehabilitating his second.

19. Jackson and Lamprecht, ibid.

20. Marni Epstein-Mervis, "Le Corbusier's Forgotten Design: SoCal's Iconic Butterfly Roof, Curbed Los Angeles," Dec. 14, 2014, https://la.curbed.com/2014/12/24/10009160/le-corbusiers-forgotten-invention-socals-iconic-butterfly-roof-1.

opposite:

LANCE GERBER

Frey House II (1963)

photographed 2023
ARCHITECT: Albert Frey
Courtesy of *Palm Springs Life*

NORTH   SHORE   BEACH   MOTEL   SALTON   SEA

MODERNISM ON THE DESERT SHORES:
NORTH SHORE YACHT CLUB AND
THE REMAKING OF THE SALTON SEA

Luke Leuschner

Thirty miles east of Palm Springs, the gas stations, urban sprawl, and date palms unexpectedly convert to shoreline. The asphalt gets grayer, the views open up, and the Salton Sea—that wasteland of salt crust, failed postwar dreams, and art installations—dominates the landscape for over thirty-five miles.

This sense of desolation is amplified when one comes to Marina Drive, the turnoff to the North Shore Beach and Yacht Club [OPPOSITE; PP. 128–129]. Dead palm trees and sun-bleached real estate signs flank a stark path to the Club that Albert Frey designed in 1958, one of his most inventive and fantastical designs. The structure is a bizarre, metaphorical combination of sand and sea that is as anomalous as the Salton Sea itself.

A little over fifty years before construction of the Yacht Club, the Salton Sea, as we know it, did not exist. Water had been an intermittent presence in the Salton Sink since prehistoric times, although it was dry when the first white settlers seized on the agricultural potential of the lakebed.[1] In 1904, an engineering failure diverted the entire flow of the Colorado River into the Salton Sink. For the next two years, the agricultural settlement was inundated until an engineering solution rediverted the river back into the Gulf of California, leaving behind the Salton Sea.[2]

In the decades following the Sea's emergence, a few recreational and boating facilities rose along the shores, but its reputation as a destination for beach leisure was slow to develop. During World War II, the Manhattan Project sponsored the dropping of 150 experimental atomic bombs in the Salton Sea area, including prototypes for the bomb that would be dropped at Hiroshima.[3] The end of the war ushered in a recreation renaissance for the region, as new middle-class prosperity propelled Californians in search of new forms of leisure.

The transformation of the Salton Sea, however, was predicated on the development of Palm Springs, which reoriented Americans' views of the desert from

opposite:

DRAWING

North Shore Beach Motel (1958)

ink on paper
ARCHITECTS: Frey & Chambers
Albert Frey papers, Architecture and Design Collection
Art, Design & Architecture Museum, University of California, Santa Barbara

"wasteland" to "wonderland." The health resorts of the 1920s had evolved into genteel retreats for America's elite, and soon, the resort city was appearing in Hollywood films and national publications. By the 1930s, it was a place where famous movie stars came to frolic.[4]

In the mid-century, Frey and other architects promulgated Palm Springs as the trendsetting resort of the West. Desert modernism climatized the "wasteland" desert environment and heightened the popular, sellable qualities of health, leisure, and celebrity. Moreover, the formerly elite glamour of modernism was extended to California's burgeoning middle class through tract developments and club memberships.[5] New cities and resorts emerged from the seemingly endless expanse of desert that surrounded Palm Springs. Ultimately, it was this spillover effect that made developments like the North Shore Yacht Club viable.

In 1957, investors Ray Ryan and Trav Rogers began acquiring land on the North Shore of the Salton Sea. Ryan, a developer in the Palm Springs area, had recently purchased and revitalized the famed El Mirador Hotel. Rogers, his associate, was a Palm Springs cowboy and friend of many celebrities.[6] The two envisioned a development on the Salton Sea's North Shore offering a marina, yacht club, commercial district, and residential neighborhood.[7]

The *Los Angeles Times* wrote of the development in 1962:

> *Here in what was once a desolate wasteland, imaginative men are carving out one of the West's most promising recreational developments. It is the North Shore Beach marine community of homes, apartments, commercial facilities, and the two-story yacht clubhouse and 400-boat marina on the shore of the azure, shimmering Salton Sea.*[8]

In July of 1958, Ryan and Rogers hired the firm of Frey and Chambers as architects for North Shore's principal buildings. The commission was appropriate for Frey, whose designs in Palm Springs had become increasingly nautical through the 1950s. His 1953 renovation of his home, Frey I, and his design for the Premiere Apartments (1957) were fantastical combinations of aluminum, corrugated fiberglass, portholes, and a general aura of sun-tanned exuberance.

Frey delivered the first design for the North Shore Yacht Club in 1958. He wrote of his vision:

> *The design of the building presented a unique opportunity. Water sports on an inland sea in the desert. A structure that would combine features of marine and desert architecture. Materials that would withstand extreme heat and dryness, bring sunlight day after day. The first floor, earth-bound, has walls of concrete block that blend with the natural colors of the desert, while the second floor floats over it like the superstructure of a ship, with decks and portholes. The materials and colors here recall the age of the speedboat.*[9]

Frey's design ultimately delivered this metaphorical ship placed atop his typical pink-hued concrete block structure. The "ship" on the upper story was flanked with walkways sheathed in yellow corrugated aluminum and decorated with nautical flags. From there, one could look out onto the luminous expanse of water, sky, and mountain—or the small kidney bean-shaped pool on the patio deck below.

Included in the clubhouse complex was Frey's design for a bait shop constructed in the same year (1959) as the clubhouse.[10] It appears that he was responsible for the design of the North Shore Beach Estates sales office (1959), a simple modern building from which view lots for $1,995 and model homes were peddled to prospective buyers. Frey also designed a model home for the adjacent North Shore Beach Estates in 1959, though this design was never built. The walls of this house were to be constructed completely of Frey's favored pink block, upon which a corrugated-aluminum roof rested and extended to form a small carport with a service yard.

The North Shore Motel (1959) was another Frey design intended to provide an affordable tourist escape. His design consisted of a small complex of two-story rectangular buildings connected by a continuous balcony sheathed in aluminum, with colorful corrugated fiberglass dividers between each guest's balcony. The defining feature, however, was to be a surfboard-shaped porte cochere that extended from the lobby and was topped with a statue of a water skier.

Frey's hotel design was simplified into a two-building complex, and earlier plans for an attached circular restaurant were abandoned. Ultimately, the hotel was built—a basic modern structure lacking his signature details—but it was so modified from Frey's plans that he was hesitant to take credit for the project. Throughout the early 1960s, North Shore Beach enjoyed immense popularity. It combined all the attractive qualities of Palm Springs—health, celebrity, modernism—with the recreation and amenities of a beach. Upon the clubhouse's opening in 1959, throngs of celebrities, tourists, and middle-class families alike enjoyed all the things promised in its glamorous advertising. This, however, was a brief moment in the sun. In the 1970s, a period of heavy rainfall and increased agricultural runoff destabilized the Salton Sea's water levels and heightened its salinity. Nearly all the transplanted fish species died, the water turned brown and salty, the sandy shores turned to crust and fish skeletons, and the smell of algae blooms and rot tainted the fresh, healing air.[11]

By the early 1980s, North Shore and most other developments were abandoned and undesirable. The Yacht Club became forlorn, graffitied, and boarded up until a re-appreciation of Frey's work and a county grant fostered its restoration in 2010.[12] However, the motel was demolished, the marina was filled in to prevent flooding, and the tourists never returned. The allure of Palm Springs once made its way to the Salton Sea; now only the smells of algae blooms occasionally waft fifty miles over and into the resort city.

In the modern imagination, the Salton Sea is an environmental disaster consigned to a corner of the California desert. Human intervention created the sea, sold the sea, and ultimately, fouled the sea. The same human intervention also subjected the surrounding desert to cycles of "wasteland to wonderland." By labeling the desert productive, recreational, or healing, it was accepted and embraced. Historically, very little changes about the actual desert environment despite human intervention. It is still home to the same venomous reptiles, unrelenting heat, and imposing landscape. With the push-button comforts of modernism, the desert could be taken in doses, and when its appeal wore off, there was always the cocktail lounge. The interventions of North Shore and other resorts made the Salton Sea into a marketable destination, but once the fish died and saltwater engulfed the observation decks, the beach was quickly abandoned in body and spirit.

A whole new generation of tourists have flocked to the Salton Sea to witness these desolate and, at times, surreal landscapes. Is another remaking of the Salton Sea underway? Is the wonderland actually the wasteland? Regardless, the North Shore Yacht Club designed by Albert Frey endures as a monument to the cycles of hope and gloom that have perturbed the Salton Sea, its history, and its future.

NOTES

1. Kim Stringfellow, *Greetings from the Salton Sea: Folly and Intervention in the Southern California Landscape, 1905–2005* (Sante Fe: Center for American Places, 2005), 6–7.

2. W. B. Crane, "The History of the Salton Sea," *Historical Society of Southern California* 9, no. 3 (1914), 215–24.

3. Stringfellow, *Greetings*, 10.

4. Lawrence Culver, *The Frontier of Leisure: Southern California and the Shaping of Modern America* (Oxford, New York: Oxford University Press, 2010), 154–55.

5. Culver, *Frontier*, 182.

6. Clark & Frey had previously designed a number of projects for Trav Rogers, including his house, commercial horse stables, and various additions since the 1930s. There was a longstanding relationship with Frey by the time Roger hired Frey and Chambers for the North Shore project.

7. While Frey and Chambers were hired to design the buildings, Ryan and Rogers had contracted the civil engineer Jack Woolley to develop the master plan of the entire development.

8. Tom Cameron, "North Shore Beach," *Los Angeles Times*, April 10, 1962.

9. Frey and Chambers, "North Shore Beach and Yacht Club," 1959, Albert Frey Papers, UC Santa Barbara: Architecture and Design Collection.

10. The hollowed remains of the bait shop are still existent at the North Shore Yacht Club immediately south of the clubhouse.

11. Stringfellow, *Greetings*, 20–21.

12. While the exterior restoration of North Shore Yacht Club largely mirrors Frey's plans, many liberties were taken with the interior and general materials. The kidney bean pool, marina, and other facilities are long gone.

ALIFORNIA ———————————————— FREY & CHAMBERS , ARCHITECTS

RC 6-59

LIFE GIVES FORM TO ARCHITECTURE:
ALBERT FREY IN THE DESERT

Michael Rotondi

The 1920s was a decade of change and mobility, geographically, intellectually, and socially. The new inventions that shaped America—airplanes, automobiles, and radios, along with the technical advances with industrial materials and construction technology—were all portals for creative minds—especially architectural minds, which are hybrids with broad interests and insatiable curiosities—to speculate.

"Why did you come to America?" I once asked Albert, as I had asked my own father. They both wanted to live in America, a place where lives could be invented, and America *was* California. Albert believed, as many other architects did, that almost anything imaginable was possible in America; it was a place to explore one's own creative freedom, in real time and at full scale. The Aluminaire House (1931) was his dissertation on the modernist principles fostered in Paris with Le Corbusier (LC). It was all that a machine for living in was proposed to be in materiality, assemblage, aesthetic, and mobility. Europe had the aesthetic down, but not the other three. Europe grew the knowledge, intelligence, and values of architecture, and America, at that time, was given the responsibility to realize the promise.

J. Krishnamurti, the spiritual teacher, in his first book *First and Last Freedom*, used a phrase that caught the attention of David Bohm, the theoretical physicist: "the observer is the observed." Our primary filter and lens for seeing, knowing, and making is us. We manifest ourselves in everything we do. Albert *was* his house [Frey House II], and I wanted my students to understand this firsthand, so I sometimes brought my students from the Southern California Institute of Architecture (SCI-Arc) to meet him.

Albert Frey was a natural teacher. In retrospect, he taught by example of his disciplinary curiosities and creative output. He viewed the world, especially in his early formative years, through the lens of an explorer with an inventive architectural mind, who seemed to believe that the best test of an idea was to construct it. He had a lot to teach, coming of age in the 1920s and '30s,

opposite:

DEWEY NICKS

Frey Performing a Yoga Handstand, c. 1996

Palm Springs Art Museum, S2017.4

one of the most significant periods of social, scientific, and technological growth in human history. Europe imagined the impact of technological ideals, and America had the real goods.

After spending an afternoon in conversation with Albert, following him with our eyes, sometimes our bodies, one of my students, who may have been a bit skeptical about the geometric simplicity of the house, made a statement:

"I never imagined a rectangle could be so interesting and complex," he said. I smiled. He and the others had been paying attention.

As we listened to Albert, he slowly moved around, giving us the opportunity to "slow look" at the house and to realize, in all its simplicity, there was a complex story distilled into its anatomy, accessible with patience and presence. We moved from inside to outside and back again as he told us stories about the house and how it came to be on the side of a mountain, and how he had to negotiate with and honor the mountain to be allowed to inhabit this place. The house was an agent for his other works, being the depository for all that had come before. It was embedded with ideas he began to explore as soon as he landed in America, drawn by a dream of a technological future only possible here, and the ideas he had brought with him from his European work experiences.

Listening to Albert talk about the house (and other projects) was like listening to an inventor with great optimism and a big idea who yearned to revitalize the way modern civilization viewed life, art, politics, and science. What was the architectural equivalent of this yearning? Albert was not a theorist per se; he was a "maker" of the highest order. His life aesthetic, values, and actions were that of a modernist. He spoke of his house in straightforward ways, and as we looked at what he spoke about, the synesthetic experience of listening, seeing, and thinking resonated in poetic ways, like a great folk song.

It seemed that any project could become a framework for solving a series of problems with both purpose and meaning. We listened to how he would define the problem simultaneously as a concept and with functional necessity. He would then explain how and why it was constructed as it was, what his choices were in principle and in particular, how constraints were turned into opportunities, and his joy of focusing on details.

As he stood against a long glass wall talking to us, we noticed the slope behind him, moving south away from us into an infinite field of yellow flower blooms. It was springtime. Upon refocusing on him, the yellow blooms entered the room. How was that possible? Albert smiled with gentle satis-faction as he noticed our startled looks. He told us he had searched for the perfect yellow curtains to match the sloped field of yellow on the mountain-side. Wow! The space of the house was relational, connected to the space of the mountain, and these choices were a duet between man and nature.

Our eyes followed him from the yellow wall on the east, as he moved to the opposite side of the room and then outside to feed a family of birds playing in a natural shallow pond in a concave rock, bathing, drinking, and pecking at the seeds Albert was lying down. They all behaved as if expecting him. This was a daily ritual, he said—late afternoon, feeding the animals who had been there longer than him. Coming back indoors he stopped in front of the big rock the house is "anchored" to. He stared at it with the look of a friend, and stories flowed, spoken as if he were in dialogue with the rock, not us. We listened in silence.

He then moved around to the narrow side at the front of the house, over-looking the valley and the long view easterly, and took small pieces of fresh fruit from a small container as he sat on a flat rock naturally shaped as a seat. To the side, there was an inch-wide crack in it. He asked us to be still as he held a piece of banana at the crack, about six inches long. Albert sat quietly and waited, and in a short while, a four-inch lizard slowly appeared, looking at Albert and then the fruit and then another long stare at Albert. Albert smiled and said, "I always forget he prefers oranges." After the lizard ate, he did a few push-ups, absorbing the midday sunlight before returning to his "cave."

We all sat quietly for a while—there was no need to talk. We glanced at each other, looking around, nodding our heads, and giving each other knowing smiles. In my silence, I thought about how pure modernist architecture was intended to be site-less, applying principles to matter, light, and space intended to be apart from the context it inhabited. After all, a machine for living in was conceived to be as adaptable as an automobile, a machine for moving in. I also thought about the three mindsets that define an architect's creative approach and intentions. Each of these may be a resident state for someone, and for another, a provisional state of being. It is possible to have a capacity for all three, situationally made manifest.

Architecture gives form to Architecture	/ no context
Architecture gives form to Life	/ context adapts
Life gives form to Architecture	/ context informs

Albert loved the desert—its space, light and lightness, subtlety, character, and perhaps most of all, how it made him feel. Architecture was his mission, and modernism was his belief system, but the desert was his muse. His architecture embodied the principles, forms, materiality, and techniques that defined modernism, but they were nuanced as they passed through the filters of his sensibilities, which seemed to be amplified by the aesthetic of the living desert. All three mindsets were in play simultaneously, I believe. The forces that shape nature and, in turn, how nature shapes us might have been at the center of Albert's curiosity. My takeaway from the experiences from many visits to see Albert was that his house was a filter and a lens for seeing what was less than visible. It was a manifestation of who he was.

Albert was humble.
Albert was generous.
Albert was patient.
Albert was a teacher.
Albert was a visionary.
Albert was a warrior.
Albert was a teacher.

Albert was a friend and mentor.

opposite:

Frey House II (1963), detail of interior yellow curtains

photographed 2023
ARCHITECT: Albert Frey
Courtesy of Radius Books

FREY HOUSE II AND PALM SPRINGS DESERT ART MUSEUM

Janice Lyle

Albert Frey's official association with the Palm Springs Desert (now Art) Museum began shortly after the one-room museum in the downtown Plaza was established in 1938. He served on the museum's board of trustees from 1941 to 1946, assuming the role of president from 1945 to 1946.[1] In the early 1950s, the board wanted to present exhibitions and offer public programs that could accommodate larger audiences in a new structure. Two firms—Williams, Williams & Williams and Clark, Frey & Chambers—worked on the new building plans between 1953 and 1958, a reflection of the collegial relationships that existed among the local architects. Over the next decades, Frey maintained his membership in and connection to the museum.

In 1986, he approached the museum's director, Morton Golden, with a proposal to bequeath Frey House II (PP. 144–161) to the institution. The director's report at the May 16 board meeting stated:

> Mr. Frey would like to bequeath his house on Palisades Drive to the museum, with the understanding that the museum would maintain the house (with $328,000 Mr. Frey would provide) and make the house available to architects and architectural students. The exterior of the house could not be changed. The museum could use the house for a staff person to live in or rent it out.… The committee discussed this proposal at length, and the [motion to accept the gift] was unanimously approved.[2]

Following this action by the board, on June 16, 1986, Frey executed a will, which provided personal gifts to his friends and a donation of early photographs of the desert area and publications to the Palm Springs Historical Society, with the rest of the estate given to the Palm Springs Desert Museum. He added some language concerning Frey House II:

> I further request that the house be maintained and made available to students of architecture as well as other architects for study and

opposite:

LANCE GERBER

Frey House II (1963)

photographed 2023
ARCHITECT: Albert Frey
Courtesy of *Palm Springs Life*

inspiration in the future. I do not desire that the house be made available to the general public; however, it should be available, by arrangements, with persons in the field of architecture and to continue to be used as a private residence under the auspices of the Desert Museum. The contents of the house pertaining to architecture such as drawings, utensils and equipment, photographs and films, books and other publications and pertinent correspondence shall remain available in the house for inspection and information. I further request that the occupants of the house shall make themselves familiar with the contents and be able to locate items and answer questions by interested visitors and that the house shall be maintained in its present status in perpetuity.[3]

On June 8, 1994, just one month after I became executive director of the museum, Frey and his attorney Gillar Boyd met with me to discuss the promised bequest. Over the subsequent four years, Frey continued to welcome visitors to his house as part of the museum's educational programs on architecture and to offer advice, as the museum played its important role in the awareness of midcentury architecture within the community. Only two weeks before he died, my husband and I visited him at Frey House II with the book *Albert Frey Houses / 1 + 2* by Jennifer Golub and listened as Frey talked about the details of those projects. As we left, he stood in his doorway in his yellow pants, white shirt, and his favorite white hat waving us on our way.

Following his death on November 23, 1998, I helped organize the memorial service at the Welwood Murray Cemetery in Palm Springs and was one of the speakers that day, commenting: "Our children's grandchildren will have an opportunity to glimpse the essence of modern architecture and its relationship to the desert through Albert's generosity."[4]

The museum inherited the house as well as objects and papers not specifically given to his friends. The official appraisal, dated December 30, 1998, valued the house at $370,000.[5] Shortly after Frey's passing, architect Leo Marmol of Marmol Radziner prepared a rehabilitation and assessment report on Frey House II for use by museum management. The goal was to maintain the house and provide the experience of it as captured by Julius Shulman's 1964 photographs, which established Frey's original design intent.

The possible uses of Frey House II were outlined in a museum memo in 1999:

1. Use extra bedroom as an office for two staff
2. Use house for small groups for cultivation
3. Open house for tours one day per month

4. Use house as photo shoot for various magazines
5. Rent house to one individual who is sensitive to Frey's architectural importance
6. Use house as a site for an artist or architect in residence

The museum implemented numbers 1, 2, and 4, and explored 3 to determine how regular tours would be accepted by the neighbors. It was determined that numbers 5 and 6 involved some risk to the structure that seemed unnecessary at the time.[6]

Frey had donated many of his drawings to the University of California, Santa Barbara Architectural Collection,[7] but the museum needed to resolve the issue of the archival materials that remained in the house. Although the will stipulated that the materials remain in the home, staff and outside consultants believed that leaving the material in the house made both the house and the material vulnerable to theft, fire, and vagrants. In addition, the humidity and temperature control system in the house was inadequate for archival storage. So, the archival materials were removed and housed in the museum library and/or vault for better control and access. This also allowed the interpretation to emphasize the residential quality of the house before Frey moved his office files there in 1967. Some copies of important documents and drawings were made and then shared with visitors to the house.[8] From 1999 until 2004, the curator of natural science and/or a development officer used the bedroom in the 1972 addition as an office. However, over time, this arrangement did not seem to offer the best protection for the house, which was looking forlorn in its essentially empty state.

By September 2004, occupancy of the house was viewed as a better solution for preservation. Frey items remaining in the house were boxed and stored for possible future use. All boxed items, the filing cabinets holding business documents, and the drawings cabinet were moved to the museum and stored in an area designated as the Frey House Archives.

In October 2004, my husband Michael Boyer and I moved into Frey House II as caretakers. The opportunity to contribute intimately to the conservation of such an important house was exciting to us—we were ready for an experiment in minimalist living. We used Julius Shulman's 1964 photographs of the house as the basis for the restoration of carpets, drapes, mattresses, and fabrics for the sofas, and the placement of personal items. We wanted all visitors (we gave tours to architects with their architectural students, filmmakers, curators, design editors, writers, photographers, and historians by appointment) to have an experience that was authentic to Frey's vision.

What was it like to live there? We thought it would be special, but it turned out to be extraordinary. Because Frey House II is integrated into the mountain, there was a seamless quality between inside and out. There were days when the wind made us feel that we were camping in the middle of the desert, in a remote and private spot, with the forces of nature all around us. Once, during a storm, we were awakened by booming claps of thunder and flashes of lightning. Being inside the highest structure on the mountain—made of glass with a metal roof—during a tremendous storm was exciting. The curtains stop short of the ceiling, so we were always aware of the natural light in the sky. Usually, it was the sun that woke us as it shone directly on the bed in the morning, but that night, it was the wild and constant lightning that kept us company.

The house was like a well-designed sailboat. The sofas, table, bed, and a hidden safe next to the giant boulder are all thoughtfully built in. We became friendly with the only plumber adept at servicing a historic toilet, and we were always careful to close the sliding glass doors. The wildlife that can be observed from the house—lizards, ground squirrels, hummingbirds, and a fabulous red-tailed hawk—felt as if they were part of our family, but we were not excited about the scorpions that stung both of us.

One of my greatest discoveries was the way living there changed my desire to own things. I would see something that was wonderful and admire it but didn't have an overwhelming desire to acquire it. Where would it go?

The very small space never felt confining. The walls of glass allowed an expansiveness of spirit. Watching the colors change on the mountains at sunset offered a particularly calming experience. There was an incredible sense of peace as the pinks, purples, and browns of the mountains changed. We could hear traffic and smell barbecuing steak, and we could see the city of Palm Springs below us, but we felt separate and slower than the rest of the world. I would watch as visitors to Frey House II emerged from their cars and got their first glimpse of the house and view. I was often reminded of how that first look left me breathless, a feeling that remained with me for as long as I lived there.

In April 2007, I left my position as director of the museum and gave up my role as caretaker of the house. But the experience of living there shaped my subsequent views about what makes a home—Frey captured the elements that feed our souls.[9]

NOTES

1. Patricia Mastick Young, *Desert Dream Fulfilled: The History of the Palm Springs Desert Museum* (Palm Springs: Palm Springs Desert Museum, 1983), 75, 77.

2. Palm Springs Desert Museum board minutes for May 16, 1986. Palm Springs Art Museum Institutional Archives. Museum curator Katherine Hough remembers participating in a meeting with Albert Frey and Frederick Sleight in 1978 when Frey broached the subject of a possible donation of Frey House II.
However, no official documentation of the discussion exists and no other references to a donation were found prior to the 1986 action.

3. Albert Frey's will. Palm Springs Art Museum Albert Frey Collection 55-199.2 Series XIV-box 1, folder 1.

4. Janice Lyle Frey file. Palm Springs Art Museum Albert Frey Collection 55-199.2 Series XIV-box 1, folders 3, 4.

5. Legal filing dated December 30, 1998. Palm Springs Art Museum Albert Frey Collection 55-199.2 Series XIV-box 1.

6. Janice Lyle Frey file. PSAM Albert Frey Collection 55-199.2 Series XIV-box 1, folders 3, 4.

7. In 1988, Frey solicited the museum's approval of a request from David Gebhard, professor of architectural history at UCSB, regarding the acquisition of Frey drawings for the Architectural Collection at the school. The museum agreed that access for scholarly research would be facilitated by that donation. Then in 1992, the museum was a venue for the traveling exhibition *Albert Frey: Modern Architect* organized by UCSB; Joseph Rosa's book about Albert Frey (Rizzoli, 1990) served as a catalog. This exhibition coincided with the resurgence of interest in midcentury modern architecture, the growth of a modern preservation movement in Palm Springs, the recognition of Frey's work in national publications, and the expansion of architectural programs at the museum.

8. Janice Lyle Frey file. Palm Springs Art Museum Albert Frey Collection 55-199.2 Series XIV-box 1, folders 3, 4.

9. Personal notes by Janice Lyle for presentation at the Walk of Stars dedication for Albert Frey on February 12, 2010. Magazine articles by Lyle for *Palm Springs Life*, February 2006; *Modernism*, Winter 2007-08; *Hauser*, March 2007; and *Plaisirs de Vivre*, June-July 2008. Palm Springs Art Museum Institutional Archives.

TEA WITH MR. FREY

Christina Kim

For a few years, I had a too-quiet store on a side street in Telluride with a view across a rough field to Ajax Mountain, the big mountain with the mines, not the mountain with the ski lifts. The store had little foot traffic, and whenever someone did come around, we'd inevitably end up in long, winding conversation. One day, a woman came in by herself. I remember her big smile. We got to talking. Her name was Jennifer Golub. We discovered that we shared things in common, including a connection to Los Angeles and an interest in architecture. Jennifer told me she was working on a book about the two houses Albert Frey built for himself in Palm Springs, Albert Frey Houses I and II. She nudged me to visit Mr. Frey when I was in LA and gave me his number. I called Mr. Frey, dropped Jennifer's name, and organized a visit, scheduled for June 15, 1998.

I drove to Palm Springs in my silver 1970 BMW 2800CS. It's the car I still use today. I got to the Frey house—perched above the town on the base of the San Jacinto massive, anchored to its granite boulder, simultaneously modest and remarkable—at 11 am. I drove up the winding drive to the parking below the house. Mr. Frey greeted me from the top of the steps with a sparkle in his eyes wearing long, slim pink pants and an old, but well cared for, Lacoste t-shirt.

Mr. Frey said he was impressed that I'd driven through Joshua Tree to get to Palm Springs. He shared his love of cars, declared mine "not bad," and invited me in. I immediately fell in love with the choice of materials; the mélange of translucent creams, off-orange, and celadon in his galley kitchen, which opened to the living room, and its sweeping, yellow curtain that Mr. Frey said was the color of brittle bush blossoms. He told me he wanted that color around all year. Surfaces—plywood, corrugated fiberglass—had been softly faded by desert light. Sitting in the interior reminded me of sitting in the rock outcroppings at Joshua Tree. Our talk of cars led Mr. Frey to tell of first landing in America and his drive west. He asked if I would like to swim while he practiced yoga and took a little nap. Sure!

opposite:

LANCE GERBER

Frey House II (1963) dinnerware

photographed 2023
ARCHITECT: Albert Frey
Courtesy of *Palm Springs Life*

One hour or so later, Mr. Frey asked if I could make us cups of tea. Lipton never looked so elegant, poured into the Eva Zeisel teacups with saucers. We talked about the different paths, in life and in our travels, each of us had taken. Much of our talk seemed to be about how it was we had come to be where we were and how "place" informed what we had become in life. Mr. Frey talked about Switzerland and asked about traditional Korean architecture. We shared our love for the wide, horizontal California desert landscape.

In the midst of it all, I asked him, "Where would you live if you had a choice?" After a bit of silence, he answered, "Procida," a volcanic island off of Napoli!

He wrote that out on a little note. I put the note on my dash and drove back to Los Angeles on the 10, headed into the warm, setting desert sun. To this day, the image of his trembling hand writing "Procida" brings warmness to my heart.

above:

CHRISTINA KIM

Frey House II (1963), cup with saucer, kitchen cabinet, and yellow curtains

photographed 1998
ARCHITECT: Albert Frey
Courtesy of and © Christina Kim

opposite:

Hand-drawn map by Christina Kim

includes a note about Procida, the place Albert Frey told her he would live if he had the choice during her visit to Frey House II (1963) in 1998
Courtesy of and © Christina Kim

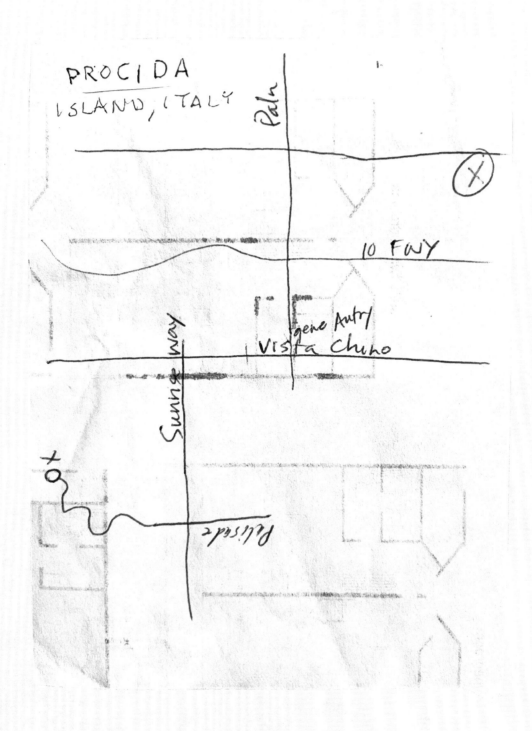

PROCIDA
ISLAND, ITALY

Palm

10 FWY

Sunny way

gene Autry
Vista Chino

Palised

built-in storage to create space in the tiny 800-square-foot home. The overall effect of Frey House II's interior is one of precision and customization: a purposeful machine built for living and working.

What a relief it must have been for the architect to break away from the conventions of Swiss climate-driven materials: concrete and thick wood planks. In the California desert, lightweight structural materials that would be deemed flimsy in the Alps are possible, and while there is something liberating and American in the freedom to be eccentric and break conventions, the work ethic it takes to so precisely engineer every detail of the building's exterior and interior—in addition to the meticulousness and thoroughness necessary to find durable and cost-effective solutions—is very Swiss.

Decades earlier, in 1931, Albert Frey and Lawrence Kocher created a concept for a house using aluminum, a then-new material, for the entire structure and exterior surfaces. The material also gave the project its name: the Aluminaire House. The furniture was made of edgy plastic sheets, inflatable thermoplastic polyurethane, and other new-to-the-world materials. It was exhibited at MoMA and, for me, shows the insatiable pursuit of material innovation from the very first years Albert Frey arrived in America.

As an immigrant and designer from Switzerland, I remember the very American acceptance of new ideas as a liberating turning point in my creative life. Yet, my Swissness remains the only way to make new ideas real, to explore them fully, to realize them with a high degree of conscientiousness and perfectionism. Much like a Swiss watch, Frey House II is highly personal, expressing a lifetime of experimentation and refinement. It works both functionally and poetically. And, in both instances, they are impossible not to fall in love with.

On my second visit to Frey House II, the Palm Springs Art Museum kindly offered me the opportunity to spend three days and three nights in the master's home. Everything about my experience was magical; the landscape around me was alive every moment of the day. While walking in the rocky mountainous surrounding area, the house almost disappeared, its small size and copacetic materials and colors making this giant of a design blend and then slowly vanish back into nature. Frey's work exemplifies the greatest achievement of good architecture and design, his object—his home—magically withdrawing from view, forever creating a long-lasting and profound memory.

225

ARCHITECTURAL RECORD 1931
A. LAWRENCE KOCHER & ALBERT FREY

C

A

TERRACE
18'-0" X 17'-0"

CL

CL

BED R
11'-0" X 8'-9"

THE EVOLUTION OF THE ARCHITECTURAL FORM:
FROM *IN SEARCH OF A LIVING ARCHITECTURE* (1939)

Albert Frey

Form is the physical realization of an inner concept. Any individual form, therefore, is dependent on an intention and exists by the presence of a purpose. Experience shows that it continues to endure if the purpose continues. When the motivation, whether practical or spiritual, ceases or takes a new course, the form degenerates, decays and finally disappears. Form variations and combinations are as countless as the thought processes that produce them. Generated by life, these efforts evolve with its evolution.

In the development of architectural form, first attempts concern themselves almost entirely with the bare materialization of an idea. Once this has been accomplished satisfactorily, attention shifts to the improvement of appearance. Creative expression reaches its climax when shape, space, and composition satisfy completely the practical requirements and interpret them in a design of intrinsic harmony.

The beauty of such expression attains one of clarity of shape, and the harmony, that of balanced co-ordination. Significance and the pleasing proportion of form are closely related to physical reality. The dimension of space or objects intended for human use are minimal., normal, or monumental in relation to one constant: the size of the man. Mass of a building part, whether structure or partition, achieves good proportion when the material used determines the dimensions. Grotesque forms are apt to result when this principle is neglected.

Any externalization of a thought eventually comes to be accepted as a matter of course and creative interest in it develops toward the more subtle occupation of spiritual enjoyment. When this happens, the practical demands are often overlooked. If in the course of development, someone finds a better and timelier expression for them, the new solution tends to

opposite:

ARTICLE

"Housing Unit Composition"

Architectural Record, 1931
ARCHITECTS: A. Lawrence Kocher with Albert Frey
Palm Springs Art Museum
Albert Frey Collection, 55-1999.2, VE1-5

supersede the original form. The use that brought about the original remains as a connotation, but since we have dispensed with active participation in it, our appreciation becomes purely intellectual and emotional, a spiritual exercise or relaxation. Mental connotation, too, gradually diminishes, and when this is fully extinguished, imitation of the form, lacking the control of practicality, sinks into mere ornament, a hinderance rather than a stimulation to the development of idea and thought. This control of form is well illustrated in nature. Trees, streams, flowers, mountains all justify themselves in terms of purpose as well as beauty.

Necessity dictates a skill in the original achievement of a form that cannot be duplicated by later imitators. The creative technique of our time goes into the production of objects derived from present conditions, not into the copies of traditional form. Continuation of conventional solutions that have become obsolete only retards natural progress ub tge establishment of expressive contemporary design. Acceptance of the inevitable change is slow because new designs demand intellectual effort while conventional patterns possess the advantage of familiarity based on habit.

Almost always the material element of an innovation receives immediate favor because it brings greater comfort, and adoption is not an effort but a convenience. For this reason, new products are often made desirable by preserving the old and customary appearance combined with the physical advantages of the modern development. Then step by step, the form is changed without the sudden break that would incur unaccustomed mental concentration. Finally people become used to and accept a new appearance that has evolved until it is fully expressive of the new mediums and conditions. Appropriate education and explanation of form evolution will speed up the process of assimilation and make possible the simultaneous creation of modern means and respective forms.

228

Often the attempt is made to compensate the lack of understanding of new shapes by terms that generalize the variegated aspects of modern products into an easily identifiable style, characteristic of some. When this happens, the result is faddish pattern superimposed on new objects indiscriminately. Discovery of newer possibilities and dissatisfaction with inappropriate adaptations force stylized fads into frequent changes, and the monotony which ensues from the unrestricted use of a fashionable form precipitates such changes into extreme reversals. Gradually, however, the most adequate expression of each product evolves and the individualized shapes which result present stimulating contrasts that make general reversals unnecessary.

It is as much a mistake to transfer aspects of modern technics, without the presence of a similar problem, as to imitate the crystallized compositions of nature or old architecture. It is by studying the forms of nature, which have always inspired mankind, and those of traditional architecture, which have endured beyond practical usefulness, for theories of idea and structure that we will discover the basic principles which guide the creation of shape, space, and composition and be able to build a living architecture that not only provides us with physical comfort but spiritual enjoyment as well.

PROJECT LISTING | 1925-1997

In his career as an architect, Albert Frey designed projects for a variety of clients in a variety of offices. Some projects are large and well known, but many are not. This project list attempts to capture the full breadth of his career and is compiled based on a number of resources, including the Frey archives at the Palm Springs Art Museum and University of California, Santa Barbara, the A. Lawrence Kocher archives at the Colonial Williamsburg library, the Palm Springs Historical Society, and other institutions.

An integral resource in compiling this list was the project index that Frey maintained throughout his career. When the architectural historian Joseph Rosa was writing his 1990 book, Frey annotated this list—which mostly covers his time in Palm Springs—with the projects that he was in charge of design for. As with any architectural office, other partners such as John Porter Clark and Robson Chambers oversaw their own projects. Just because a project emerged from Clark & Frey or the Clark, Frey & Chambers firm does not mean it was designed by Albert Frey. As Rosa explains:

> To assist me with my research on Frey's West Coast work, he augmented a copy of the office project list to identify which projects he either oversaw the design of or reflected his architectural vocabulary. This delineation allowed me to then go visit with his other partners (John Porter Clark and Robson Chambers) separately to review how Frey identified these projects that he was in-charge of. Both Clark and Chambers concurred that Frey's augmentation of the office project list was correct.[23]

Moreover, Frey's annotations included a delineation between projects he designed and projects that he designed and felt expressed his "philosophy of architecture." Those judgements are replicated here as they were listed by Frey.

This list does not attempt to capture Frey's entire career—with time comes new discoveries and understandings. It does, however, seek to deliver the most comprehensive overview to date.

— LUKE LEUSCHNER AND BRAD DUNNING

O   INDICATES ALBERT FREY WAS IN
    CHARGE OF DESIGN.

●   INDICATES ALBERT FREY WAS IN
    CHARGE OF DESIGN
    AND WAS PERMITTED TO
    EXPRESS HIS PHILOSOPHY OF
    ARCHITECTURE.

A   5019   ADAMS, B. C. (House Alteration)
    4576   O   ADAMS, F. C. (House)
    4581   ADAMS, R. R. (House)
    4834   AIKEN, DR. WM. P. (House Addition, Araby)
    4817   ALBERT, MRS. F. W. (House Plans, Smoke Tree)
    5029   O   ALSCHULER, MR. & MRS. ERNEST (Awing Addition)
    4656   AMERICAN LEGION BUILDING (M-CLARK)
    4030   ●   ANDERSON (Skating Rink)
    4739   ANDREWS, F. A. (House)
    4121   ANIMAL SHELTER
    4514   O   ARCHER-BONBRIGHT (Ranch) ADDITION
    4554   ARMSTRONG, H. W. MRS. (House)
    4626   ARMSTRONG, H. W. MRS. (House Alteration)
    4648   ARMSTRONG, H. W. MRS. (Kitchen Alteration)
    4768   O   ARMSTRONG, H. W. MRS. (House Additions, Smoke Tree
                                                              Ranch)
    5031   ARMSTRONG, H. W. MRS. (Awning Addition)

ALBERT FREY PARTNERSHIPS AND OFFICES

1926–27:   Eggericx & Verwhilgen (draftsman)

1927–28:   Leuenberger & Fluckinger (draftsman)

1928–29:   Le Corbusier and Pierre Jeanneret (draftsman)

1929–30:   Eggericx & Verwhilgen (designer)

1930–35:   A. Lawrence Kocher

1931–32:   William Lescaze (Howe & Lescaze) (designer)

1934:   US Department of Agriculture (designer)

1935–37:   John Porter Clark (Van Pelt & Lind)

1937–39:   Philip Goodwin (designer)

1938:   A. Lawrence Kocher

1939–52:   John Porter Clark (Clark & Frey)

1952–57:   John Porter Clark and Robson Chambers (Clark, Frey, & Chambers)

1957–66:   Robson Chambers (Frey & Chambers)

FREY'S KEY FOR THE FOLLOWING LISTING

○ — indicates that Albert Frey was in charge of design

● — indicates that Albert Frey was in charge of design
and permitted to execute his philosophy of architecture

opposite:

List of Albert Frey projects, date unknown

includes Frey's handwritten system of open and closed
circles he used to designate his relationship to each project.
This system is replicated in the project listing that follows.

1925

Frey Family Garage Addition
Zurich, Switzerland
UNBUILT

1927

Concrete Parking Tower
UNBUILT

Factory of Glass and Steel
UNBUILT

Villa Savoye, 1928

Drawing for the Frey Family
Garage Addition, 1925

Villa Church, Ville d'Avray, 1928
[Interior recreation of the music pavilion]

1928

Asile Flottant

In the offices of Le Corbusier and Pierre Jeanneret
Seine River, Paris, France
[Worked on details and drawings]
Plans for restoration as of 2023

Centrosoyuz Administration Building

In the offices of Le Corbusier and Pierre Jeanneret
Myasnitskaya Ulitsa,
39, Moscow, Russia
[Worked on presentation model, renderings, and drawings]

Housing for the Old

UNBUILT (COMPETITION)

Maison Loucheur

In the offices of Le Corbusier and Pierre Jeanneret
[Frey worked on details and drawings]
UNBUILT

Minimal Metal House

UNBUILT

Palace of the League of Nations

In the offices of Le Corbusier and Pierre Jeanneret
Geneva, Switzerland
[Frey worked on details and drawings]

Prager Factory

In the offices of Le Corbusier and Pierre Jeanneret
UNBUILT

Villa Church

In the offices of Le Corbusier and Pierre Jeanneret
1 Avenue Halphen, 92410 Ville-d'Avray, France
[Frey worked on details and drawings]
DEMOLISHED

Villa Savoye

In the offices of Le Corbusier and Pierre Jeanneret
82 Rue de Villiers,
78300 Poissy, France
[Frey worked on construction drawings and contributed to the design
of windows and sliding glass doors, bathroom chaise, and other details]

1929

Cité de Refuge

In the offices of Le Corbusier and Pierre Jeanneret
12 Rue Cantagrel, 75013 Paris, France
[Frey worked on details and drawings]

Mundaneum

In the offices of Le Corbusier and Pierre Jeanneret
Geneva, Switzerland
[Frey worked on details and drawings]

Office Building

In the offices of Eggericx and Verwhilgen
Brussels, Belgium
[Frey worked on details and drawings]
UNBUILT (COMPETITION)

Aluminaire House, 1930

1930

Aluminaire House

In partnership with A. Lawrence Kocher
Grand Central Palace, New York, New York;
144 Round Swamp Road, Syosset, New York;
New York Institute of Technology, School of Architecture,
Central Islip, New York; Palm Springs Art Museum,
Palm Springs, California (present location)

Darien Guild Hall

In partnership with A. Lawrence Kocher
Darien, Connecticut
UNBUILT

Farmhouse "A" and "B", 1931

Master Plan of Bukavu

In the offices of Eggericx and Verwhilgen
Bukavu, Democratic Republic of the Congo
UNBUILT

Master Plan of Uvira

In the offices of Eggericx and Verwhilgen
Uvira, Democratic Republic of the Congo
UNBUILT

Miniature Golf Course

In partnership with A. Lawrence Kocher
UNBUILT

Ralph-Barbarin House, 1932

Miniature Golf Course, 1930

Weekend House, 1932

1931

Downyflake Doughnut Shop
In partnership with A. Lawrence Kocher
Rhode Island
UNBUILT

Farmhouse "A" and "B"
In partnership with A. Lawrence Kocher
UNBUILT

Museum of Modern Art, Schemes 5 and 6
In the offices of William Lescaze (Howe and Lescaze)
New York, New York
[Frey worked on design and renderings]
UNBUILT

1932

Chrystie-Forsyth Street Housing Project
In the offices of William Lescaze (Howe and Lescaze)
Chrystie Street and Forsyth Street, New York, New York
UNBUILT

Five-Room House
In partnership with A. Lawrence Kocher
UNBUILT

River Gardens Housing Project
In the offices of William Lescaze (Howe and Lescaze)
New York, New York
[Frey worked on preliminary design]
UNBUILT

Weekend House
In partnership with A. Lawrence Kocher
UNBUILT

Ralph-Barbarin House
In partnership with A. Lawrence Kocher
71 Interlaken Road, Stamford, Connecticut

1933

Gut-Frey House
Rebbergstrasse 41, 8049 Zurich, Switzerland

Kocher-Samson Building, 1934

1934

Farmhouses No. 6531 and 6532
Under supervision of Wallace Ashby
UNBUILT

House of Prefabricated Walls and Floors
In partnership with A. Lawrence Kocher
UNBUILT

Kocher Canvas Week-End House
In partnership with A. Lawrence Kocher
Meadow Glen Road, Northport, Long Island, New York
DEMOLISHED

Kocher-Samson Building
In partnership with A. Lawrence Kocher
766 North Palm Canyon Drive, Palm Springs, California

Low-Cost House
In partnership with A. Lawrence Kocher
UNBUILT (COMPETITION)

Subsistence Farmsteads
In partnership with A. Lawrence Kocher
UNBUILT

Farwell House, 1936

1935

Brandenstein Study ●

In partnership with John Porter Clark (Van Pelt and Lind)
287 East Morongo Road, Palm Springs, California
DEMOLISHED

Foss Construction House ○

In partnership with John Porter Clark (Van Pelt and Lind)
415 East Valmonte Norte, Palm Springs, California
STATUS UNDETERMINED

Guthrie House ●

In partnership with John Porter Clark (Van Pelt and Lind)
666 East Mel Avenue, Palm Springs, California

Lorenzo Apartments [Hotel San Jacinto] ●

In partnership with John Porter Clark (Van Pelt and Lind)
726 North Indian Canyon Drive, Palm Springs, California

Rogers House ○

In partnership with John Porter Clark (Van Pelt and Lind)
Palm Springs, California
STATUS UNDETERMINED

Guthrie House, 1935

1936

Farwell House ●

In partnership with John Porter Clark (Van Pelt and Lind)
1120 East Balboa Boulevard, Newport Beach, California
Addition in 1940

Halberg House ●

In partnership with John Porter Clark (Van Pelt and Lind)
775 East Mel Avenue, Palm Springs, California

Kellogg Studio and Addition ○

In partnership with John Porter Clark (Van Pelt and Lind)
321 West Vereda Sur, Palm Springs, California
Alteration in 1941

La Siesta Bungalow Court ●

In partnership with John Porter Clark (Van Pelt and Lind)
247 West Stevens Road, Palm Springs, California

Steel House ○

In partnership with John Porter Clark (Van Pelt and Lind)
Lake Arrowhead, California
STATUS UNDETERMINED

Halberg House, 1936

1937

Museum of Modern Art

In the offices of Philip Goodwin and Edward Durrell Stone (Goodwin and Stone)
11 West 53rd Street, New York, New York
[Frey designed the lecture hall and reading room, window and door details, and modifications to street facade, including rooftop circular cutouts]

Mason Duplex ●

In partnership with John Porter Clark
448 East Cottonwood Road, Palm Springs, California
STATUS UNDETERMINED

Swiss Pavilion at New York World's Fair, 1938

1938

Festival Theatre and Fine Arts Center

In the offices of Philip Goodwin (Goodwin and Stone)
College of William and Mary, Williamsburg, Virginia
UNBUILT (COMPETITION)

Swiss Pavilion at New York World's Fair

In partnership with A. Lawrence Kocher
Flushing Meadows-Corona Park, Queens, New York
UNBUILT (COMPETITION)

1939

A. Guthrie House ○

Clark & Frey, 650 North Via Miraleste, Palm Springs, California
STATUS UNDETERMINED

Boyd House Addition ○

Clark & Frey, 216 West Via Lola, Palm Springs, California
STATUS UNDETERMINED

Dellside Dairy ●

UNBUILT (COMPETITION)

Chamber of Commerce ●

Clark & Frey, Palm Springs, California
UNBUILT

Chaney Apartments ●

Clark & Frey, 275 Tamarisk Road, Palm Springs, California

Nellie Coffman Middle School Shop Building ●

Clark & Frey, 34603 Plumley Road, Cathedral City, California
DEMOLISHED

Blue Lagoon Recreation Project, 1940

Chaney Apartments, 1939

1939 (cont.)

Risk Guest House ○

Clark & Frey, Palm Springs, California
STATUS UNDETERMINED

Smithsonian Gallery of Art

In the offices of Philip Goodwin (Goodwin, Jaeger, and Frey Associates)
Washington, D.C.
UNBUILT (COMPETITION)

1940

Blue Lagoon Recreation Project

Clark & Frey, Palm Springs, California
UNBUILT

Cathedral City Elementary School ●

Clark & Frey, Van Fleet Street, Cathedral City, California
ADDITIONS IN 1946, 1947, 1948, AND 1951, DEMOLISHED

El Mirador Cocktail Room ○

Clark & Frey, 1150 North Indian Canyon Drive, Palm Springs, California
DEMOLISHED

F. D. Johnson House ○

Clark & Frey, Smoke Tree Ranch, Palm Springs, California
ADDITIONS IN 1972, 1980, AND 1982

Frey House I ●

1210 North Via Donna, Palm Springs, California
ADDITIONS IN 1947, 1953, 1964, 1972, AND 1987, ALTERED

Garland House ○

Clark & Frey, Palm Springs, California
STATUS UNDETERMINED

Hill House ●

Clark & Frey, 877 West Panorama Road, Palm Springs, California

Johnson Bungalows ○

Clark & Frey, 269 East Chuckwalla Road, Palm Springs, California

Lone Palm Court Addition ○

Clark & Frey, 1276 North Indian Canyon Drive, Palm Springs, California
ADDITIONS IN 1941, 1945, 1946, AND 1947, DEMOLISHED

Nellie Coffman Middle School Addition ●

Clark & Frey, 34603 Plumley Road, Cathedral City, California
ADDITIONS/ALTERATIONS IN 1942, 1945, 1948, AND 1957, DEMOLISHED

1940 (cont.)

Oasis Hotel Bungalows ○

Clark & Frey, 125 South Palm Canyon Drive, Palm Springs, California
DEMOLISHED

Palm Springs Bowl Roller Rink ●

Clark & Frey, Sunrise Way and Ramon Avenue, Palm Springs, California
DEMOLISHED

Palm Springs City Gates ●

Clark & Frey, Highway 111, Palm Springs, California
DEMOLISHED

Welwood Murray Memorial Library ●

Clark & Frey, Palm Springs, California
UNBUILT

Palm Springs City Gates, 1940

1941

Cahuilla Elementary School ●

Clark & Frey, 833 East Mesquite Avenue, Palm Springs, California
ADDITIONS IN 1945, 1946, 1947, 1953, AND 1957, DEMOLISHED

El Mirador Hotel Shop Interior ○

Clark & Frey, 1150 North Indian Canyon Drive, Palm Springs, California
DEMOLISHED

Markham House ●

Clark & Frey, Smoke Tree Ranch, Palm Springs, California
ADDITIONS IN 1950 AND 1983

Merwin House ○

Clark & Frey, Smoke Tree Ranch, Palm Springs, California
ADDITIONS IN 1945, 1950, 1952, 1960, 1970, AND 1971

Palm Springs Health Center ●

Clark & Frey, 459 East Amado Road, Palm Springs, California
DEMOLISHED

Palm Springs Water Company Building ●

Clark & Frey, 844 North Palm Canyon Drive, Palm Springs, California

Sieroty House ●

Clark & Frey, 695 East Vereda Sur, Palm Springs, California
ALTERATION IN 1988

Simsarian Store ●

Clark & Frey, 824 North Palm Canyon Drive, Palm Springs, California
DEMOLISHED

Frey House I, 1940

1942

American Airlines Terminal ●

Clark & Frey, Palm Springs Airport, Palm Springs, California
UNBUILT

Burritt House ●

Clark & Frey, Smoke Tree Ranch, Palm Springs, California
ADDITION IN 1960

El Mirador Hotel to Torney General Hospital Conversion ○

Clark & Frey, 1150 North Indian Canyon Drive, Palm Springs, California
DEMOLISHED

J. Wells House ●

Clark & Frey, Smoke Tree Ranch, Palm Springs, California
ADDITIONS IN 1947, 1968, 1974, AND 1983

Kellogg House ○

Clark & Frey, Phoenix, Arizona
UNBUILT

Jaeger House ○

Clark & Frey, Palm Springs, California
UNBUILT

Sayler House Addition ○

Clark & Frey, 483 West Via Sol, Palm Springs, California
STATUS UNDETERMINED

1943

Homeowners Loan Corporation Housing Modifications ○

Clark & Frey, Various properties in Riverside and Orange County
STATUS UNDETERMINED

Zalud House Addition ○

Clark & Frey, 216 West Camino Descanso, Palm Springs, California
STATUS UNDETERMINED

1944

Gholstin House ○

Clark & Frey, 538 South Indian Trail, Palm Springs, California

Jacobson House ○

Clark & Frey, Palm Springs, California
UNBUILT

Schlothan House Alteration ○

Clark & Frey, 478 West Merito Place, Palm Springs, California
STATUS UNDETERMINED

J. Wells House, 1942

1945

Adams House ○

Clark & Frey, 845 West Chino Canyon Road, Palm Springs, California

Armstrong House ○

Clark & Frey, Smoke Tree Ranch, Palm Springs, California
ADDITIONS IN 1946 AND 1947
STATUS UNDETERMINED

Bel Vista War Housing ●

Clark & Frey
1111, 1127, 1128, 1133, 1134, 1149, 1150, 1163, 1164, 1179, 1180, and 1193
North Calle Rolph, & 1520 East Tachevah Drive, Palm Springs, California

Bill House ○

Clark & Frey, 623 West Chino Canyon Road, Palm Springs, California

Breske House ●

Clark & Frey, Palm Springs, California
UNBUILT

Browne Development ○

Clark & Frey, Palm Springs, California
UNBUILT

Campbell Duplex ●

Clark & Frey, Palm Springs, California
UNBUILT

Chamberlin Building ○

Clark & Frey, 469 North Palm Canyon Drive, Palm Springs, California
DEMOLISHED

Cree House I ●

Clark & Frey, 442 Hermosa Place, Palm Springs, California
ADDITION IN 1946
DEMOLISHED

Crommelin House

Clark & Frey, Smoke Tree Ranch, Palm Springs, California
ADDITION IN 1960

Hatton House and Guest House, 1945

Doll House Restaurant Addition ●

Clark & Frey, 1032 North Palm Canyon Drive, Palm Springs, California
DEMOLISHED

Dozier House ○

Clark & Frey, Indio, California
STATUS UNDETERMINED

Nelson House, 1945

Filice and Perrelli House Addition ○

Clark & Frey, 953 North Avenida Palmas, Palm Springs, California
STATUS UNDETERMINED

Fleet House ○

Clark & Frey, Palm Springs, California
UNBUILT

Florsheim House Addition ○

Clark & Frey, 688 East Vereda Del Sur, Palm Springs, California
ADDITION IN 1957
STATUS UNDETERMINED

Hatton House and Guest House ●

Clark & Frey, 22 Tennis Club Drive, Rancho Mirage, California
DEMOLISHED

Harper House ○

Clark & Frey, 330 West Stevens Road, Palm Springs, California
DEMOLISHED

Hopkins Duplex ○

Clark & Frey
STATUS UNDETERMINED

Hormel House Addition ○

Clark & Frey, 840 North Prescott Drive, Palm Springs, California
ALTERATION IN 1979
STATUS UNDETERMINED

Kemper House Addition

Clark & Frey, Palm Springs, California
UNBUILT

Kirk House Addition ○

Clark & Frey, 335 Camino Norte, Palm Springs, California
STATUS UNDETERMINED

McDougall House Addition ○

Clark & Frey, 271 West Merito Place, Palm Springs, California
STATUS UNDETERMINED

Morongo Lodge Addition ○

Clark & Frey, Morongo Valley, California
STATUS UNDETERMINED

Nelson House ●

Clark & Frey, Indio, California
UNBUILT

Nelson Studio ●

Clark & Frey, Monroe Avenue, Indio, California
STATUS UNDETERMINED

1945 (cont.)

Nichols Building Addition ●

Clark & Frey, 861 North Palm Canyon Drive, Palm Springs, California
ALTERATIONS IN 1948, 1952, 1957, 1971, AND 1972

Palm Springs Food Locker Alteration ○

Clark & Frey, 311 South Palm Canyon Drive, Palm Springs, California
STATUS UNDETERMINED

Powell House Addition ●

Clark & Frey, 383 Vereda Del Norte, Palm Springs, California
Additions in 1947, 1951, and 1989
STATUS UNDETERMINED

Racquet Club Guest Bungalows ●

Clark & Frey, 2743 North Indian Canyon Drive, Palm Springs, California

Satlitz and Baker Duplex ○

Clark & Frey, Camino Real, Palm Springs, California
STATUS UNDETERMINED

Schlothan Hotel Alteration [Pepper Tree Inn] ○

Clark & Frey, 645 North Indian Canyon Drive, Palm Springs, California
STATUS UNDETERMINED

Strieby House ●

Clark & Frey, Palm Springs, California
UNBUILT

Stutz Duplex ●

Clark & Frey, Palm Springs, California
UNBUILT

Van Heusen House ●

Clark & Frey, Yucca Valley, California
UNBUILT

Villa Hermosa ●

Clark & Frey, 155 Hermosa Place, Palm Springs, California
ALTERATIONS IN 1947 AND 1961

Wahl House Addition

Clark & Frey, Vista Chino, Palm Springs, California
STATUS UNDETERMINED

Wilbor Bungalows ○

Clark & Frey, Yucca Valley, California
UNBUILT

Woolley House I ●

Clark & Frey, 856 East Paseo El Mirador, California

Villa Hermosa, 1945

Loewy House, 1946

1946

Colgan Apartments [Chuckwalla Manor] ●
Clark & Frey, 269 East Chuckwalla Road, Palm Springs, California
ADDITIONS IN 1956 AND 1966

Cooper House ●
Clark & Frey, 2360 South Araby Drive, Palm Springs, California

Cree Office Alteration ○
Clark & Frey, 285 North Palm Canyon Drive, Palm Springs, California
DEMOLISHED

Desert Hot Springs Elementary School ●
Clark & Frey, Palm Drive and 2nd Street, Desert Hot Springs, California
DEMOLISHED

Frances Stevens School Alteration ○
Clark & Frey, 550 North Palm Canyon Drive, Palm Springs, California
STATUS UNDETERMINED

Haight House ○
Clark & Frey, Palm Springs, California
STATUS UNDETERMINED

Loewy House ●
Clark & Frey; Raymond Loewy, 600 Panorama Road, Palm Springs, California

Lone Palm Court Bungalows ●
Clark & Frey, 1276 North Indian Canyon Drive, Palm Springs, California
UNBUILT

McFarland Apartment ●
Clark & Frey, 409 North Palm Canyon Drive, Palm Springs, California

Nelson Guest House ●
Clark & Frey, Indio, California
UNBUILT

Pacific Building Alteration ●
Clark & Frey, 789 North Palm Canyon Drive, Palm Springs, California
ALTERATION IN 1953, STATUS UNDETERMINED

Racquet Club Addition ●
Clark & Frey, 2743 North Indian Canyon Drive, Palm Springs, California
ADDITIONS IN 1946, 1947, 1948, 1949, 1950, 1951, 1957, AND 1961
STATUS UNDETERMINED

1946 (cont.)

Samson Building [Desert Clinic] ●

Clark & Frey, 760 North Palm Canyon Drive, Palm Springs, California
ALTERATION IN 1960

Seeburg Building ●

Clark & Frey, 1087 North Palm Canyon Drive, Palm Springs, California
ADDITIONS/ALTERATIONS IN 1951 AND 1959

Waale-Camplan Co. and Smith Inc. Building ●

Clark & Frey, Palm Springs, California
DEMOLISHED

Waale-Camplan Co. and Smith Inc. Building ●

Clark & Frey, Los Angeles, California
STATUS UNDETERMINED

Zalud Stables ●

Clark & Frey, Beaumont, California
UNBUILT

Zanuck House Alteration ○

Clark & Frey, 346 Tamarisk Road, Palm Springs, California
UNBUILT

Dollard Building, 1947

1947

Clark & Frey Building ●

Clark & Frey, 879 North Palm Canyon Drive, Palm Springs, California

Cree Ranch House ●

Clark & Frey, Palm Springs, California
UNBUILT

Desert Hills Hotel ●

Clark & Frey, Cathedral City, California
UNBUILT

Dollard Building ●

Clark & Frey, 687 North Palm Canyon Drive, Palm Springs, California

Gilmore House Addition ●

Clark & Frey, Smoke Tree Ranch, Palm Springs, California
ADDITIONS/ALTERATIONS IN 1954, 1956, 1965, 1969,
1977, 1980, 1981, 1982, 1984, 1989, AND 1990

Hamrick House Addition ○

Clark & Frey, 875 West Chino Canyon Road, Palm Springs, California
STATUS UNDETERMINED

Imes House Addition   O

Clark & Frey, Palm Springs, California
STATUS UNDETERMINED

Isenagle House Alteration   O

Clark & Frey, 1028 East San Jacinto Way, Palm Springs, California
STATUS UNDETERMINED

Levy House   O

Clark & Frey, Palm Springs, California
UNBUILT

Livingston House   O

Clark & Frey, Palm Springs, California
UNBUILT

Nichols House Alteration   O

Clark & Frey, East Paseo El Mirador, Palm Springs, California
STATUS UNDETERMINED

Paddock Pool Company Building

Clark & Frey [John Porter Clark, lead architect]
693 Ramon Road, Palm Springs, California

Purcell Office Addition   O

Clark & Frey, 700 North Palm Canyon Drive, Palm Springs, California
STATUS UNDETERMINED

Rosenthal House   ●

Clark & Frey, Palm Springs, California
UNBUILT

San Gorgonio Pass Memorial Hospital   ●

Clark & Frey, 660 North Highland Springs Avenue, Banning, California

Somalia House   O

Clark & Frey, Palm Springs, California
STATUS UNDETERMINED

Stutz Apartments   ●

Clark & Frey, Palm Springs, California
UNBUILT

Willard Pool Building   ●

Clark & Frey, Palm Springs, California
STATUS UNDETERMINED

San Gorgonio Pass Memorial Hospital, 1947

1948

American Legion Post #519

Clark & Frey [John Porter Clark, lead architect]
400 North Belardo Road, Palm Springs, California

Besser House   O

Clark & Frey, Smoke Tree Ranch, Palm Springs, California
ADDITIONS IN 1974, 1980, 1981, AND 1982

Cortissoz House   ●

Clark & Frey, 71346 Sahara Road, Rancho Mirage, California
DEMOLISHED

Desert Bank   ●

Clark & Frey, 68435 Highway 111, Cathedral City, California
DEMOLISHED

El Mirador Hotel Restoration   O

Clark & Frey, 1150 North Indian Canyon Drive, Palm Springs, California
DEMOLISHED

Hoover House Addition   O

Clark & Frey, Smoke Tree Ranch, Palm Springs, California
ADDITIONS/ALTERATIONS IN 1951, 1984, 1986, AND 1993
STATUS UNDETERMINED

Jennings House   ●

Clark & Frey, Palm Springs, California
UNBUILT

Lyman House Addition   O

Clark & Frey, 829 North Patencio Road, Palm Springs, California
DEMOLISHED

Lyons House   ●

Clark & Frey, Smoke Tree Ranch, Palm Springs, California
ADDITIONS IN 1972 AND 1981

North End School [Katherine Finchy Elementary School]   ●

Clark & Frey, 777 East Tachevah Drive, Palm Springs, California
DEMOLISHED

Maloney House   O

Clark & Frey, Kalamazoo, Michigan
UNBUILT

Sanders House Addition   O

Clark & Frey, Smoke Tree Ranch, Palm Springs, California
STATUS UNDETERMINED

Turner House

Clark & Frey, Smoke Tree Ranch, Palm Springs, California
ADDITIONS IN 1950, 1956, AND 1986

Wells House   ●

Clark & Frey, Rancho Mirage, California
UNBUILT

American Legion Post #519, 1948

North End School (Katherine Finchy), 1948

1949

"D" Street Elementary School Addition ●
Clark & Frey, 500 D Street, Needles, California

Essex Elementary School Addition ●
Clark & Frey, Needles, California
STATUS UNDETERMINED

Halberg House II ○
Clark & Frey, Port Angeles, Washington
UNBUILT

Henderson House Addition ○
Clark & Frey, 844 North Mission Road, Palm Springs, California
STATUS UNDETERMINED

Le Gro Guest House ○
Clark & Frey, 354 West Stevens Road, Palm Springs, California
STATUS UNDETERMINED

Needles Junior High School Addition ●
Clark & Frey, 700 Bailey Avenue, Needles, California
STATUS UNDETERMINED

Tobin House ●
Clark & Frey, Port Angeles, Washington
UNBUILT

Turonnet Building ●
Clark & Frey, 707-745 North Palm Canyon Drive, Palm Springs, California
ADDITION IN 1949

Vista Colorado Elementary School ●
Clark & Frey, 700 Bailey Avenue, Needles, California

1950

Alschuler House Addition ○
Clark & Frey, 421 Santa Rosa Drive, Palm Springs, California
STATUS UNDETERMINED

Benoist Guest House ●
Clark & Frey, 385 Alta Vista Road, Palm Springs, California

Boyd Ranch Barbecue ●
Clark & Frey, Deep Canyon, Palm Desert, California
STATUS UNDETERMINED

Desert Hospital ●
Clark & Frey; Williams, Williams, and Williams
1150 North Indian Canyon Drive, Palm Springs, California

Desert Bank, 1948

Desert Hospital, 1950

1950 (cont.)

Desert Bank Renovations ●
Clark & Frey, 456 North Palm Canyon Drive, Palm Springs, California
DEMOLISHED

Palm Springs Fire Station ●
Clark & Frey, 480 South Sunrise Way, Palm Springs, California
ALTERED

Social Sciences and Humanities Building,
University of California, Riverside ●
Clark & Frey, Watkins Hall, University of California, Riverside

Welwood Murray Memorial Library Addition ○
Clark & Frey, 100 South Palm Canyon Drive, Palm Springs, California
STATUS UNDETERMINED

Palm Springs Fire Station, 1950

1951

Brecher House
Clark & Frey, 723 East Vereda Sur, Palm Springs, California

Committee of 25 Clubhouse Addition ○
Clark & Frey, 412 West Alejo Road, Palm Springs, California
ADDITIONS IN 1951, 1958, AND 1959, STATUS UNDETERMINED

Dollard House ●
Clark & Frey, Rancho Mirage, California
DEMOLISHED

Joy House ●
Clark & Frey, 73355 Grapevine Street, Palm Desert, California
DEMOLISHED

Lockwood House ○
Clark & Frey, Pasadena, California
STATUS UNDETERMINED

Ohrbach House ○
Clark & Frey, Palm Springs, California
UNBUILT

Parker Dam School ●
Clark & Frey, California Street and Utah Street, Parker Dam, California
DEMOLISHED

Pelletier House ●
Clark & Frey, 73297 Grapevine Street, Palm Desert, California

Rogers Ranch Club Alterations ○

Clark & Frey, 1600 East Chia Road, Palm Springs, California
DEMOLISHED

Schwabacher House ○

Clark & Frey, Jackson Hole, Wyoming
STATUS UNDETERMINED

Turonnet House Addition ○

Clark & Frey, 734 North Prescott Drive, Palm Springs, California
DEMOLISHED

1952

Cahuilla Elementary School Multi-Purpose Building ●

Clark, Frey, & Chambers, 833 Mesquite Avenue, Palm Springs, California
DEMOLISHED

Le Gro House Addition ○

Clark, Frey & Chambers, 354 West Stevens Road, Palm Springs, California
STATUS UNDETERMINED

Palm Springs City Hall ●

Clark, Frey & Chambers; Williams, Williams, and Williams
3200 East Tahquitz Canyon Way, Palm Springs, California

Scholl House Addition ○

Clark, Frey & Chambers
211 East Morongo Road, Palm Springs, California
STATUS UNDETERMINED

Warren House ○

Clark, Frey & Chambers
Palm Springs, California
UNBUILT

Social Sciences and Humanities Building,
University of California, Riverside, 1950

Palm Springs City Hall, 1952

1953

Benoist House Addition ●

Clark, Frey & Chambers
ADDITIONS IN 1956 AND 1989, STATUS UNDETERMINED

Desert Museum ●

Clark, Frey & Chambers; Williams, Williams, and Williams
125 East Tahquitz Canyon Way, Palm Springs, California
ADDITION IN 1960, DEMOLISHED

Farrell House Addition ○

Clark, Frey & Chambers, 630 East Tachevah Drive, Palm Springs, California
ADDITIONS IN 1956 AND 1962, STATUS UNDETERMINED

Pacific Building Alteration ○

Clark, Frey & Chambers, 798 North Palm Canyon Drive, Palm Springs, California
STATUS UNDETERMINED

Schwabacher House Addition ○

Clark, Frey & Chambers, 368 West El Portal, Palm Springs, California
ALTERATION IN 1960, STATUS UNDETERMINED

West House Addition ○

Clark, Frey & Chambers, 414 East Valmonte Sur, Palm Springs, California
STATUS UNDETERMINED

Woolley House II ○

Clark, Frey & Chambers, 1055 East Paseo El Mirador, Palm Springs, California

Banning Library, 1954

1954

Banning Library

Clark, Frey & Chambers, 21 West Nicolet Street, Banning, California

Banning Union High School Library ●

Williams, Clark, and Frey, 100 West Westward Avenue, Banning, California
ADDITION IN 1960, DEMOLISHED

Carlson House ○

Clark, Frey & Chambers, 521 West Linda Vista Drive, Palm Springs, California
ADDITION IN 1987, STATUS UNDETERMINED

Carpenter House Addition ○

Clark, Frey & Chambers, 333 West Merito Place, Palm Springs, California
ADDITION IN 1958, STATUS UNDETERMINED

Henderson House Addition ○

Clark, Frey & Chambers, 4 Warm Sands Place, Palm Springs, California
STATUS UNDETERMINED

Hinton House ●

Clark, Frey & Chambers, 9420 La Jolla Shores Drive, La Jolla, California

Cree House II, 1955

Hinton House, 1954

Palm Springs Fire Station No. 1, 1955

Thompson Apartment Hotel, 1957

1955

Cielo Vista Elementary School •

Clark, Frey & Chambers, 650 South Paseo Dorotea, Palm Springs, California

Hill House [Cree II] •

Clark, Frey & Chambers, 67389 East Palm Canyon Drive, Cathedral City, California

James House O

Clark, Frey & Chambers, Palm Desert, California
UNBUILT

Palm Springs Fire Station No. 1 O

Clark, Frey & Chambers, 277 North Indian Canyon Drive, Palm Springs, California

1956

Carey House •

Clark, Frey & Chambers, 651 West Via Escuela, Palm Springs, California
ADDITIONS IN 1983 AND 1992

First Church of Christ, Scientist

Clark, Frey & Chambers, 605 South Riverside Drive, Palm Springs, California

Hull House Addition O

Clark, Frey, & Chambers, 2311 North Indian Canyon Drive, Palm Springs, California
STATUS UNDETERMINED

Slaughter Building

Clark, Frey & Chambers, 250 East Palm Canyon Drive, Palm Springs, California
DEMOLISHED

1957

Bernet House Addition •

Frey & Chambers, 1163 North Calle Rolph, Palm Springs, California
STATUS UNDETERMINED

Burgess House Addition

Frey & Chambers, 550 Palisades Drive, Palm Springs, California
ADDITIONS/ALTERATIONS IN 1967, 1968, 1974, 1978, 1982, 1984, 1986, & 1987

Cree Site Plan and Houses •

Frey & Chambers, Cathedral City, California
UNBUILT

Foursquare Gospel Church [Desert Chapel] •

Frey & Chambers, 630 Vella Road, Palm Springs, California

Thompson Apartment Hotel [Premiere Hotel Apartments] •

Frey & Chambers, 190 West Baristo Road, Palm Springs, California;
261 Belardo Road, Palm Springs, California (relocated in 1972)
DEMOLISHED

1958

Nellie Coffman Middle School Multi-Purpose,
Music, and Administration Building ●
Frey & Chambers, 34603 Plumley Road, Cathedral City, California
ADDITION IN 1960, DEMOLISHED

North Shore Yacht Club ●
Frey & Chambers, 99155 Sea View Drive, Mecca, California

North Shore Yacht Club Boat Rental Building ●
Frey & Chambers, 99155 Sea View Drive, Mecca, California

Palm Springs High School Shop Building ●
Frey & Chambers, 2248 East Ramon Road, Palm Springs, California

Saint Michael's By-The-Sea Episcopal Church
Frey & Chambers, 2775 Carlsbad Avenue, Carlsbad, California
ADDITION IN 1964

North Shore Yacht Club, 1958

1959

American Red Cross Riverside County Chapter House ●
Frey & Chambers, 8880 Magnolia Avenue, Riverside, California

Frelinghuysen House Addition ●
Frey & Chambers, 707 West Panorama Road, Palm Springs, California
STATUS UNDETERMINED

Haskin House Addition ○
Frey & Chambers, 2427 North Tuscan Road, Palm Springs, California
STATUS UNDETERMINED

North Shore Beach Estates Homes ●
Frey & Chambers, North Shore, Mecca, California
UNBUILT

North Shore Beach Estates Sales Office
Frey & Chambers, North Shore, Mecca, California
DEMOLISHED

North Shore Beach Motel ○
Frey & Chambers, 99311 Sea View Drive, Mecca, California
DEMOLISHED

Physical Science Building, College of the Desert ○
Frey & Chambers; John Carl Warnecke Associates
College of the Desert, Palm Desert, California

Ryan House ●
Frey & Chambers, Bermuda Dunes, California
UNBUILT

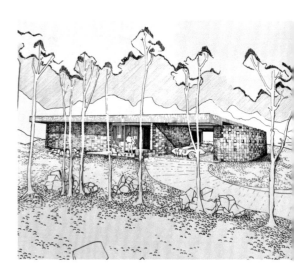

Drawing for North Shore Beach Estates Homes, 1959

Saint Michael's By-The-Sea
Episcopal Church, 1958

1960

Alpha Beta Food Market (Beaumont) ○
Frey & Chambers, 1400 Beaumont Avenue, Beaumont, California
DEMOLISHED

Alpha Beta Food Market (Indio) ●
Frey & Chambers, 81850 Highway 111, Indio, California
DEMOLISHED

Alpha Beta Food Market (Palm Springs) ●
Frey & Chambers, 425 South Sunrise Way, Palm Springs, California
DEMOLISHED

Monkey Tree Hotel
Frey & Chambers, Palm Springs, California
UNBUILT

Schiff House Addition ●
Frey & Chambers, 2743 North Indian Canyon Drive, Palm Springs, California

1961

Alpha Beta Food Market (Claremont) ○
Frey & Chambers, Claremont, California
STATUS UNDETERMINED

Alpha Beta Food Market (Santa Ana) ○
Frey & Chambers, 2521 West McFadden Avenue, Santa Ana, California

Clark House Addition
Frey & Chambers, Smoke Tree Ranch, Palm Springs, California
STATUS UNDETERMINED

De Anza Country Club Clubhouse ●
Frey & Chambers, Borrego Springs, California
UNBUILT

Palm Springs High School Addition ●
Frey & Chambers, 2248 East Ramon Road, Palm Springs, California
STATUS UNDETERMINED

Alpha Beta Food Market (Palm Springs), 1960

1962

Lund and Guttry Office Alteration ○
Frey & Chambers, Palm Springs, California
STATUS UNDETERMINED

Nichols Building I ●
Frey & Chambers, 891-899 North Palm Canyon Drive, Palm Springs, California

Nichols Chino Canyon Hotel ●
Frey & Chambers, Tramway Road, Palm Springs, California
UNBUILT

Nichols Neighborhood Shopping Center ●
Frey & Chambers, Tramway Road, Palm Springs, California
UNBUILT

Nichols Restaurant ●
Frey & Chambers, Tramway Road, Palm Springs, California
UNBUILT

Palm Springs Aerial Tramway Valley Station ●
Frey & Chambers, Tramway Road, Palm Springs, California

Steinmeyer House ●
Frey & Chambers, 318 West Pablo Drive, Palm Springs, California

Palm Springs Aerial Tramway Valley Station, 1962

1963

Palm Canyon Ranch Development ○
Frey & Chambers, Palm Springs, California
UNBUILT

Frey House II ●
686 Palisades Drive, Palm Springs, California
ADDITION IN 1972

Hollingsworth House I ●
Frey & Chambers, 187 West San Marco Way, Palm Springs, California
UNBUILT

La Quinta Country Club Clubhouse Alteration ●
Frey & Chambers, La Quinta, California
UNBUILT

Sillano House ○
Frey & Chambers, Desert Hot Springs, California
UNBUILT

Smallman House ○
Frey & Chambers, Palm Springs, California
STATUS UNDETERMINED

Three Keys Development ○
Frey & Chambers, Palm Springs, California
UNBUILT

Nichols Service Station [Tramway Gas Station], 1965

1964

Armstrong House O

Frey & Chambers, Smoke Tree Ranch, Palm Springs, California
UNBUILT

Hi-Desert Memorial Hospital O

Frey & Chambers, Yucca Valley, California
UNBUILT

Milner House Addition O

Frey & Chambers, 447 West Alejo Road, Palm Springs, California
STATUS UNDETERMINED

Palm Canyon Mall O

Palm Springs Planning Collaborative, Palm Springs, California
UNBUILT

Post Office and Federal Building O

Frey & Chambers, 200 East Murphy Street, Banning, California

Thornton House

Frey & Chambers, Smoke Tree Ranch, Palm Springs, California
ADDITIONS IN 1969 AND 1971, STATUS UNDETERMINED

Wahl House ●

Frey & Chambers, Lake Tahoe, California
UNBUILT

1965

Doinwick House O

Frey & Chambers, Palm Springs, California
STATUS UNDETERMINED

Fisher House Addition O

Frey & Chambers, 375 West Vista Chino, Palm Springs, California
STATUS UNDETERMINED

Palm Valley School Addition O

Frey & Chambers, 35535 Da Vall Drive, Rancho Mirage, California
STATUS UNDETERMINED

Saunders House Addition O

Frey & Chambers, 421 West Mariscal Road, Palm Springs, California
STATUS UNDETERMINED

Shell Oil Company Gas Station ●

Frey & Chambers, 900 North Palm Canyon Drive, Palm Springs, California
DEMOLISHED

Nichols Service Station [Tramway Gas Station] ●

Frey & Chambers, 2901 North Palm Canyon Drive, Palm Springs, California

1966

Brennan House ●
3820 Esther Way, Teton Village, Wyoming

Brennan House Addition ●
Smoke Tree Ranch, Palm Springs, California
STATUS UNDETERMINED

Hollingsworth House II ●
155 West San Marco Way, Palm Springs, California
ADDITION IN 1976

Lund House
Cherry Valley, California
UNBUILT

Newton House I ●
Palisades Drive, Palm Springs, California
UNBUILT

1967

Burgess Guest House ●
550 Palisades Drive, Palm Springs, California

Gilmore House ●
Smoke Tree Ranch, Palm Springs, California

Moore House Addition ●
Smoke Tree Ranch, Palm Springs, California
ADDITION IN 1982, STATUS UNDETERMINED

Owens House Addition ○
Smoke Tree Ranch, Palm Springs, California
STATUS UNDETERMINED

Smoke Tree Ranch Clubhouse Addition ●
Smoke Tree Ranch, Palm Springs, California
Additions in 1969, 1983, and 1993
STATUS UNDETERMINED

Smoke Tree Ranch Condominiums
Smoke Tree Ranch, Palm Springs, California
UNBUILT

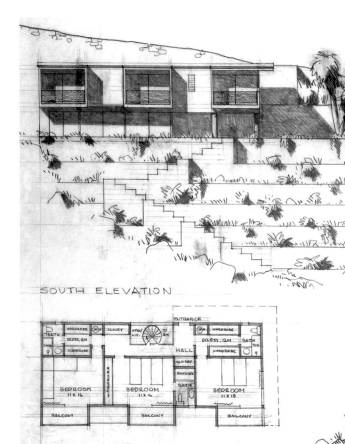

Newton House I, 1966

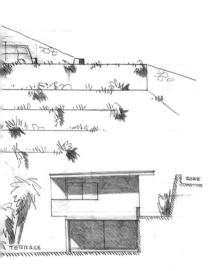

1968

Nichols Building II ○

1200 North Palm Canyon Drive, Palm Springs, California

Newton House II

698 West Ramon Road, Palm Springs, California
UNBUILT

Schiff Ranch House

La Quinta, California
UNBUILT

1969

Brunner House ○

Teton Village, Wyoming
STATUS UNDETERMINED

1970

L. Merwin House Addition

Smoke Tree Ranch, Palm Springs, California
STATUS UNDETERMINED

1971

NO DOCUMENTED PROJECTS

1972

NO DOCUMENTED PROJECTS

1973

Moore House Addition ●

Smoke Tree Ranch, Palm Springs, California
ADDITIONS/ALTERATIONS IN 1976, 1980, AND 1983

Sawyer House Addition

Smoke Tree Ranch, Palm Springs, California
STATUS UNDETERMINED

Wasserman House Interior

Palm Springs, California
UNBUILT

1974

Siva Pool Pavilion

200 West Vereda Sur, Palm Springs, California
UNBUILT

Ryan House

Smoke Tree Ranch, Palm Springs, California
ADDITION IN 1975

Wolfe House Alteration

Idyllwild, California
ALTERATIONS IN 1976, 1987, 1994

1975

Shane House Addition

501 Santa Rosa Drive, Palm Springs, California
UNBUILT

Wasserman House Alteration

1011 West Cielo Drive, Palm Springs, California

1976

Evans House Addition

2240 East Smokewood Avenue, Palm Springs, California
ADDITIONS/ALTERATIONS IN 1976 AND 1978,
STATUS UNDETERMINED

F. Supple House Addition

Smoke Tree Ranch, Palm Springs, California
ADDITIONS IN 1985 AND 1995, STATUS UNDETERMINED

Skelton House Addition

Spring Crest, Mountain Center, California
STATUS UNDETERMINED

1977

Beirne House Addition

395 South Patencio Road, Palm Springs, California
ADDITION IN 1979

Lilley House Addition

Smoke Tree Ranch, Palm Springs, California
ADDITIONS IN 1979, 1985, AND 1988, STATUS UNDETERMINED

Phinny Guest House and Studio

Smoke Tree Ranch, Palm Springs, California
STATUS UNDETERMINED

Smoke Tree Ranch Guest Cottages

Smoke Tree Ranch, Palm Springs, California
ALTERATION IN 1979

Terhune House Addition

2300 Palermo Drive, Palm Springs, California
ADDITIONS IN 1978 AND 1986, STATUS UNDETERMINED

1978

Rose House Addition

1053 San Lucas Road, Palm Springs, California
STATUS UNDETERMINED

Terhune Guest House

2300 Palermo Drive, Palm Springs, California
UNBUILT

Tyler House Addition

Smoke Tree Ranch, Palm Springs, California
ADDITION IN 1985, STATUS UNDETERMINED

1979

C. Supple House Addition

Smoke Tree Ranch, Palm Springs, California
STATUS UNDETERMINED

Hoffman House Addition

Smoke Tree Ranch, Palm Springs, California
ADDITION IN 1988, STATUS UNDETERMINED

Hankins House Alteration

840 Prescott Drive, Palm Springs, California
STATUS UNDETERMINED

Rawn House Addition

Smoke Tree Ranch, Palm Springs, California
STATUS UNDETERMINED

1980

Bryant House Addition

Smoke Tree Ranch, Palm Springs, California
UNBUILT

Phinny House

Smoke Tree Ranch, Palm Springs, California
UNBUILT

Phinny House Addition

Smoke Tree Ranch, Palm Springs, California
ADDITIONS IN 1984 AND 1985, STATUS UNDETERMINED

Richmond House Addition

Smoke Tree Ranch, Palm Springs, California
STATUS UNDETERMINED

Sherwin House Addition

Smoke Tree Ranch, Palm Springs, California
ADDITION IN 1984, STATUS UNDETERMINED

1981

Davis House Addition

2222 Del Lago Road, Palm Springs, California

Harpham House Addition

Smoke Tree Ranch, Palm Springs, California
STATUS UNDETERMINED

1982

Russell House Additions

660 Palisades Drive, Palm Springs, California

1983

Burgess Guest House

550 Palisades Drive, Palm Springs, California
UNBUILT

Lawrence House Addition

Smoke Tree Ranch, Palm Springs, California
STATUS UNDETERMINED

Nichols Tourist Center

Tramway Road, Palm Springs, California
UNBUILT

Smoke Tree Ranch Offices

Palm Springs, California
STATUS UNDETERMINED

Wilson House Addition

Smoke Tree Ranch, Palm Springs, California
ADDITIONS IN 1983, 1985, AND 1986, STATUS UNDETERMINED

Yantis House Addition

296 West Hermosa Place, Palm Springs, California
STATUS UNDETERMINED

Yates House Alteration

Smoke Tree Ranch, Palm Springs, California
STATUS UNDETERMINED

1984

NO DOCUMENTED PROJECTS

1985

Bauman House Alteration

1105 East Cactus Road, Palm Springs, California
STATUS UNDETERMINED

Broderick House Addition

289 South Via Las Palmas, Palm Springs, California
STATUS UNDETERMINED

Firring House Addition

2065 Tulare Drive, Palm Springs, California

Gordon House Addition

829 Inverness Drive, Rancho Mirage, California
STATUS UNDETERMINED

Green House Addition

Smoke Tree Ranch, Palm Springs, California
STATUS UNDETERMINED

Ivers Cabin

Pinyon Crest, Mountain Center, California
UNBUILT

Moore House Addition

Smoke Tree Ranch, Palm Springs, California
STATUS UNDETERMINED

Shea House Addition

1690 Ridgemore Drive, Palm Springs, California
STATUS UNDETERMINED

Vaughan House Addition

Smoke Tree Ranch, Palm Springs, California
STATUS UNDETERMINED

DRAWING

Burgess Mirrored Pavilion (1986)

pencil on paper
ARCHITECT: Albert Frey
Palm Springs Art Museum
Albert Frey Collection

1986

Embury House Addition
530 West Tahquitz Canyon Way, Palm Springs, California
STATUS UNDETERMINED

Frenzel House Addition
501 North Cantera Circle, Palm Springs, California
STATUS UNDETERMINED

Marston House Addition
2350 Araby Drive, Palm Springs, California
STATUS UNDETERMINED

Burgess Mirrored Pavilion
550 Palisades Drive, Palm Springs, California

Owens House Addition
2103 Rim Road, Palm Springs, California
STATUS UNDETERMINED

1987

NO DOCUMENTED PROJECTS

1988

Cravens House
Smoke Tree Ranch, Palm Springs, California

Lehman House Addition
Smoke Tree Ranch, Palm Springs, California
STATUS UNDETERMINED

Newgard House Addition
974 La Jolla Road, Palm Springs, California

1989

NO DOCUMENTED PROJECTS

Burgess Mirrored Pavilion, 1986

Vacation Cottage, 1997

1990

Di Pietra House Addition

789 East Racquet Club Road, Palm Springs, California

Durgom House Addition

333 West Via Sol, Palm Springs, California

Foster House Alteration

943 Avenida Olivos, Palm Springs, California
STATUS UNDETERMINED

Harris House

Rim Rocks Drive, Cathedral City, California
UNBUILT

Frink House Alteration

1230 Via Monte Vista, Palm Springs, California
STATUS UNDETERMINED

1991

Chandler House Addition

Thunderbird Heights, Rancho Mirage, California
STATUS UNDETERMINED

1992–1994

NO DOCUMENTED PROJECTS

1995

Dunning-Magnuson Patio Remodel

Los Angeles, California
UNBUILT

1997

Vacation Cottage

UNBUILT

While giving a private tour of Frey House II once to family friends vacationing in Palm Springs, it occurred to me that Albert Frey's gifts are not obvious to everyone. Based on the confused look in their eyes, it was clear they were expecting something more typically elegant and refined. With all the luxurious modern homes in Palm Springs, I can understand how they would expect the grandfather of desert modernism to design a house for himself that was glamorous or stately. And that's not where Frey's genius lies. That's not the reason he is so beloved by architects and architecture aficionados around the world. Frey built for himself a small house with a poured concrete floor and concrete block and corrugated aluminum walls on the exterior. Except for the giant boulder in the center, which has its own kind of modesty as part of the existing landscape, it doesn't come off as very ambitious. Here the grandfather of architecture, in a city known for its images of celebrities in posh modern homes, designs modest buildings with inexpensive materials, which border on being bohemian. His gifts stem from his inventiveness and insight into how to use what he has. His genius is that he makes it look as if he isn't even trying.

I lived at Frey House II for six weeks, and I never got tired of seeing the boulder in the middle of the space. Every time I walked into the house, it would imprint on me. I would wake up in the morning, Hello, Boulder. I would look up from reading a book, Boulder. It never receded into the environment. A shift in the angle of the house one direction, and it would have. It would have become a wall. A shift in the other direction, it would have been an aggressive imposition into the space. As it is, it feels like a gesture, a gift given over and over again. The entire space, nestled into the side of the mountain with expansive views of the valley, is designed to make nature palpable. Characteristic of Frey's modesty, he allows nature to deliver her gifts.

Despite my experience with my family friends, I am gratified to see that younger generations have the eyes to see Frey's achievements. It makes sense that they are rediscovering him. His sensibility aligns perfectly with a cohort interested in upcycling, tiny houses, and van life. He is a guiding spirit for people who care more about authentic living than owning things.

Frey is the grandfather we want. He reminds us that the desert is not just a place of escape—it's a place of possibility. It's a place where it is possible to take knowledge and traditions from elsewhere and replant them, allowing them to take shape in a new way.

Fame favors the self-promoters of the world, but time tends to reveal the genuine inventors. I trust this book and its accompanying exhibition will help give Frey his due.

— ADAM LERNER

JoAnn McGrath Executive Director / CEO, Palm Springs Art Museum

ACKNOWLEDGMENTS

There are many people to thank for helping make this project possible. Most importantly, we are grateful to the title sponsors of this book, Roland Lewis & Michael Noll, and presenting sponsor, the Palm Springs Preservation Foundation.

Thanks to our lead sponsors James Gaudineer & Tony Padilla, Brent R. Harris & Lisa K. Meulbroek & The Harris Charitable Trust, Geoffrey De Sousa & José Manuel Alorda, Elizabeth Edwards Harris, Roland Lewis & Michael Noll, *Palm Springs Life*, The Sam & Diane Stewart Family Foundation, Trina Turk, and Stephen Winters & Don Curtis. Additional funding provided by L. J. Cella, Mimi & Steve Fisher, Joan & Gary Gand, Arthur Keller & Mark Gauthier, Eric Kranzler, Tobias Meyer & Mark Fletcher, Douglas Moreland, Julie Rogers, Ronnie Sassoon & James Crump, Christine & Jim Scott, Bonnie Serkin & Will Emery, and Jim & Kathy Simpson.

The museum is incredibly grateful to Brad Dunning for his inexhaustible devotion to Albert Frey and this project. His vast knowledge of the subject is matched only by the intensity of his curiosity and his commitment to representing Frey accurately and splendidly.

Many thanks to the museum staff who have done so much to make this book and exhibition happen, especially Rachael Faust, Director of Collections and Exhibitions, whose efficiency and administrative finesse are unparalleled.

We are especially grateful to Dave Chickey and the team at Radius Books for their belief in this endeavor and their ability to make an awesome book.

We are grateful to Palm Springs Art Museum board of trustees for their ongoing commitment to the Architecture and Design program, especially to L. J. Cella and Leo Marmol, who have been among the most vocal, hardworking, and generous advocates on the board.

We also need to thank the mighty community of architecture lovers in Palm Springs who have done so much over the years to preserve the legacy of modern architecture that Frey helped establish.

— ADAM LERNER

ACKNOWLEDGMENTS

I am indebted and grateful for so many who helped make this exhibition and book possible and assisted and encouraged me along the way:

Louis Grachos, former director of the Palm Springs Art Museum, who invited me to curate this exhibition; Luke Leuschner, the best research historian and rabbit hole co-explorer one could hope for; Frank Lopez, the intrepid, patient, and knowledgeable archivist at Palm Springs Art Museum; Rachael Faust, Director of Collection & Exhibitions, Palm Springs Art Museum, who miraculously kept it all together for all of us involved; Adam Lerner, JoAnn McGrath Executive Director/CEO Palm Springs Art Museum, the captain of the ship, without whose support and enthusiasm for the exhibition it would not have happened; David Chickey, Nick Larsen, Mat Patalano, Megan Mulry, and Isabella Beroutsos at Radius Books; Tom Johnson, Palm Springs Art Museum's stalwart, creative, and can-do-anything exhibition designer; Larry Hochanadel, exhibition construction contractor extraordinaire; L. J. Cella, Board of Directors, Palm Springs Art Museum, navigator, friend, diplomat, and get-things-done wizard behind the curtain; Sidney Williams, all-seeing, all-knowing, all-supporting oracle of all things past and present Palm Springs Art Museum; Marianne Martin, Visual Resources Librarian, John D. Rockefeller Jr. Library, Colonial Williamsburg Foundation; Silvia Perera, Curator, Architecture and Design Collection, University of California, Santa Barbara; The Palm Springs Preservation Foundation, who enthusiastically supported the exhibition and book from the very beginning; Brent R. Harris and Lisa Meulbroek, friends, professors, and patrons supreme; Bijan Fahimian, the great miniaturist, our patient and meticulous architectural modelmaker; Julie Rogers, moral support and general angel do-gooder; Frank Jones, owner, *Palm Springs Life* magazine, for his constant and steadfast support of the exhibition; Stephen Mark Johnston, draftsman, architectural designer, and technical virtuoso; Renee Brown of the Palm Springs Historical Society; Rochelle McCune of the Historical Society of Palm Desert; and The Smoke Tree Ranch Archives.

I relied heavily on the work and research of others, especially and primarily the exhaustive and academic work of Joseph Rosa. It was his 1990 book that first introduced me to Albert Frey's work, and for that and his valued friendship and support, I will be forever grateful and dedicate this exhibition to him.

And lastly, to Albert Frey, a friend and teacher, who inspired me and whose legacy I hope I have honored justly. See you on the trail.

— BRAD DUNNING

Design entrepreneur **Yves Béhar** believes that integrated product, digital, and brand design are cornerstones of any business. In 1999, Béhar founded fuseproject—a multidisciplinary, award-winning, first-in-category San Francisco agency, built on Béhar's belief that design accelerates the adoption of new ideas, including positive social and environmental change. Focused on industrial, digital, strategy, branding, and innovation, the studio's work spans from designing advanced tech and robotics solutions to smart-home technology, furniture, and environments to health offerings, as well as social and non-profit projects. In addition to receiving international acclaim for his contributions to the design field, Béhar's works are included in permanent museum collections worldwide. His monograph, *Yves Béhar: Designing Ideas*, published by Thames & Hudson, was released in 2021.

Brad Dunning is a designer, writer, and curator known for working on architecturally significant properties, restorations, and his own contemporary work. Award-winning architectural restorations include designs by Richard Neutra, Wallace Neff, John Lautner, Lutah Riggs, and Albert Frey, among many others. He has also written about design, architecture, and architectural preservation for various publications, including the *New York Times*, *Interview*, the *Los Angeles Times*, and *Vogue,* and was a long-time contributing editor on architecture and design for *GQ* magazine. He has lectured on historic preservation, Alexander Girard, Albert Frey, the Wandervögel in California, and midcentury architecture in Hawaii, among other topics. In 2021, Dunning curated *The Modern Chair* at the Palm Springs Art Museum Architecture and Design Center.

Paul Goldberger, who the *Huffington Post* has called "the leading figure in architecture criticism," is now a contributing editor at *Vanity Fair*. From 1997 through 2011, he served as the Architecture Critic for *The New Yorker*, where he wrote the magazine's celebrated "Sky Line" column. He also holds the Joseph Urban Chair in Design and Architecture at The New School in New York City. He was formerly dean of the Parsons School of Design, a division of The New School. He began his career at *The New York Times*, where in 1984 his architecture criticism was awarded the Pulitzer Prize for Distinguished Criticism, the highest award in journalism.

Forty years ago, **Christina Kim** started dosa as an artistic experiment. It was a conversation with commerce, a way to communicate through designing clothes. Through her travels, she met people and discovered collaborators, developing her ideas. Her time spent investigating and making has grown into an expansive body of work, focused on creating goods of enduring value and zero waste. Recent exhibitions include: Arumjigi Museum, Seoul; Cooper Hewitt Museum, New York; Mingei Museum, San Diego; Textile Museum, Washington, DC; Factory2, South Korea; TextielMuseum, Netherlands; Center of the Arts of San Agustin, Oaxaca; Anyang Public Art Project 5, South Korea; RISD Museum, Providence; Venice Architecture Biennale 2016; Milan Triennial 2016.

Raised in Canada and New York City, **Dr. Barbara Lamprecht** is a Pasadena-based architectural historian specializing in the rehabilitation of Modern buildings and preparing evaluations and designations. Lamprecht is the author of *Neutra: Complete Works* (Taschen, 2000), *Neutra* (Taschen 2004), and *Richard Neutra: Furniture: The Body and the Senses* (Wasmuth, 2015). Published by Atara Press, she has written a scholarly introduction to a new edition of Neutra's manifesto, *Survival Through Design*, to be released this winter. She has taught architectural history and has lectured at venues including the National Building Museum, the MoMA San Francisco, MOCA Los Angeles, ModernismWeek, and the Getty Conservation Institute. The California Preservation Foundation presented her with the 2022 President's Award for her work in expanding Neutra scholarship. Lamprecht earned an MArch at Cal Poly Pomona and her PhD at the University of Liverpool. Her dissertation explored Neutra's nineteenth- and twentieth-century roots in neuroscience, evolutionary biology, and landscape, leading to her interest in the brain/body/environment connection.

Luke Leuschner is a California-based historian focused on the state's architecture, urbanism, and identity, with a particular interest in the state's desert regions. Born and raised in Palm Desert, CA, he developed an affinity for the city's forgotten and undocumented modern architecture. This interest led him to the Historical Society of Palm Desert, where he worked (and continues to work) on a multi-year endeavor to document and archive the city's built environment. He is currently working on a book on the work of the modernist architect Rudolph Schindler in the California desert. He sits on the City of Berkeley's Landmarks Preservation Commission and is a board member of the California Garden and Landscape History Society.

Director of the Sunnylands Center & Gardens from 2008 to 2022, **Janice Lyle** oversaw the restoration of the historic Annenberg estate, the construction of the public Center & Gardens, and the building of the Sunnylands administrative campus. She managed a professional team responsible for the preservation, interpretation, and public aspects of Sunnylands. Prior to joining Sunnylands, Lyle was the executive director of the Palm Springs Desert (now Art) Museum from 1994 to 2007 and director of Public Programs for the previous ten years. She is the author of *Sunnylands: America's Midcentury Masterpiece* (Vendome, 2016); has lectured extensively on modern architecture, preservation, and museum topics; and served on numerous nonprofit boards, including as president of the California Association of Museums. Lyle received her master of arts and her PhD in art history from the University of California, Santa Barbara.

Joseph Rosa is an arts consultant with a broad background, encompassing his years as a museum director, curator, author, educator, and practicing architect. Joe was director/CEO of the Frye Art Museum in Seattle from 2016 to 2022 and the director of the University of Michigan Museum of Art from 2010 to 2016. Previously, he held curatorial department head positions at the Art Institute of Chicago, the San Francisco Museum of Modern Art, the Carnegie Museum of Art in Pittsburgh, and the National Building Museum in Washington, DC. He has curated more than fifty art and architecture exhibitions, written seventeen books, and is a noted scholar on architect Albert Frey and Julius Shulman, the highly acclaimed twentieth-century architectural photographer. Early in his career, he worked in the architecture offices of Peter D. Eisenman, Gwathmey Siegel, Tsao & McKown, and Gruen Associates.

Michael Rotondi has practiced and taught architecture locally and internationally for over forty years, always operating from his base in Los Angeles. He was a founding partner of Morphosis (1975–1991), founding principal of RoTo Architects (1991–present), and a co-founder of SCI-Arc, where he co-created and directed the graduate program (1978–1987), was the second institute director from 1987 to 1997, and currently remains distinguished faculty. He has additionally taught and lectured at many other schools, including twenty years at Arizona State University (2000–2020). Throughout four decades, practice and teaching have become complimentary halves of one activity: growing and deploying an "Architectural Mind." Although teaching has specific objectives, it can also serve as a form of research that informs the broader practice. RoTo's curiosity about "anything and everything unfamiliar, yet connected," drives a longtime passion for cross-disciplinary practice and is the basis of an open-minded approach that has attracted a wide array of clients and diverse range of projects.

Operating on the belief that the arts—all arts—are vital to our culture, RADIUS BOOKS is a 501(c)(3) non-profit organization with a focus on photography and fine art book publishing.

In addition to publishing, RADIUS BOOKS encourages aspiring artists through educational workshops and community events and distributes books of artistic and educational value for a wide audience.

RADIUS BOOKS donates copies of every title we publish into a nationwide network of libraries and schools, with the hope and expectation that these books will reach and inspire new audiences.

RADIUS BOOKS
227 E. Palace Avenue, Suite W, Santa Fe, NM 87501
t: (505) 983-4068 | radiusbooks.org

PALM SPRINGS ART MUSEUM
101 North Museum Drive, Palm Springs, CA 92262
t: (760) 322-4800 | psmuseum.org

ISBN 979-8-89018-079-7
Library of Congress Cataloging-in-Publication
Data available from the publisher upon request.

EDITOR: Brad Dunning
DESIGN & EDITORIAL: David Chickey, Nick Larsen
PUBLICATION MANAGER: Rachael Faust
ARCHIVAL PHOTOGRAPHY: Lance Gerber

Printed by Editoriale Bortolazzi-Stei, Verona, Italy

JACKET: Lance Gerber, Frey House II (1963), photographed 2023